GEORGE ROGERS CLARK

and

the War in the West

LOWELL H. HARRISON

THE UNIVERSITY PRESS OF KENTUCKY

Frontispiece:
George Rogers Clark   Portrait by Matthew Jouett
(Courtesy of The Filson Club, Louisville)

Research for The Kentucky Bicentennial Bookshelf
is assisted by a grant from the
National Endowment for the Humanities.
Views expressed in the Bookshelf do not
necessarily represent those of the Endowment.

ISBN: 0-8131-0224-3

Library of Congress Catalog Card Number: 76-4431

To Peg and Tex

Contents

Preface

THE AMERICAN REVOLUTION was fought on a small scale compared with several of the nation's later conflicts. Fewer than 7,000 soldiers died of battle wounds during more than six years of fighting, and even if those who perished in camps and British prisons are included, the total of just over 25,000 is small in relation to the size of the nation's population and the length of the struggle.

But small though it was, the war in the East dwarfed the war in the West, along the Ohio Valley. The population in the West was so scant, and the harassed new government could devote so little attention to the lands beyond the mountains, that the conflict was waged there by forces that seldom merited the designation of army. Only occasionally, and only toward the end of the Revolution, could as many as a thousand Kentucky militiamen be gathered for a brief expedition, and George Rogers Clark's most spectacular exploits were carried out with forces numbering less than two hundred men.

The war in the West differed from that waged in the East in another aspect also. Had the Revolution been suppressed, a few of the eastern ringleaders would probably have been executed as examples to other potential rebels, but the majority of the participants would have resumed their previous status with little disruption to their lives. In the West, however, the war was fought for survival; there was no civilian population. If the Americans living in Kentucky were defeated, their lives were likely to be lost—unless they were carried into captivity to be adopted into an Indian tribe or sold to British authorities for location in Canada. They could, of course, flee eastward across the mountains, a decision that would have rolled back the frontier and opened long-settled communities to attack.

Knowing as we do the outcome of the American Revolution, it is difficult to realize just how precarious was the existence of the settlements in Kentucky during the desperate years that extended well beyond the surrender of Lord Cornwallis at Yorktown. The man who did most to save Kentucky during that perilous era was George Rogers Clark. It is the purpose of this essay to show the vital role that Clark played in the phase of the Revolution that centered on Kentucky and the Illinois country.

Clark has been somewhat ignored by historians in recent years, perhaps in reaction to the hero-worshipping homage tendered him by some of his early biographers. Clark's exploits do not require romantic exaggeration; the man and his career are fascinating without the addition of myth and legend. He was the savior of Kentucky and one of the commonwealth's legitimate heroes. Unfortunately for his reputation, he lived too long, and his later failures were a pathetic aftermath to the brilliant accomplishments of his earlier years. Clark lived to be sixty-six; his reputation declined after he was thirty.

George Rogers Clark wrote two accounts of his most successful campaign, a memoir and a lengthy letter to George Mason, and the Clark quotations in the text are taken from them unless another source is indicated. The restricted format of the Bicentennial Bookshelf precludes the extensive documentation that would be required to identify each one. When Clark did not employ the services of a secretary his prose has a stream-of-consciousness quality with much use of disconnected clauses, a fine disregard for punctuation, and an erratic approach to capitalization. Most authors who have quoted from Clark's writings have made some changes for the sake of clarity; I have done the same, while making every effort to retain his meaning. Also I have used "Kentucky" to denote the area that later achieved statehood under that name, although at times there was no area legally so called.

I owe particular thanks to the staffs of the Kentucky and Helm-Cravens libraries at Western Kentucky University and The Filson Club in Louisville for their assistance during my research. The presence of the Temple Bodley collection of Clark materials at The Filson Club and the availability of the Draper Papers of the Wisconsin Historical Society on microfilm at Western Kentucky University greatly reduced the travel that otherwise would have been required.

1

THE WAR BEGINS

WHEN THE FIGHTING of the American Revolution began on the eastern seaboard in April 1775, it had little impact upon the few inhabitants of Kentucky. Although a surprisingly large number of hunters, trappers, land speculators, and other adventurers had explored the lovely lands south of the Ohio River, the first permanent settlements were just being established at Harrodsburg and Boonesborough. The settlers were more concerned with their immediate problems than they were with events occurring hundreds of miles and several weeks away.

Of particular concern were the Indians. The British did not employ the Indians in frontier warfare during the early days of the Revolution as they did during its later stages, but many of the Indians needed no encouragement to resent the intrusion of the white settler into hunting grounds that they claimed as their own. Confronted with Indian hostility, the white population of Kentucky that may have totaled as many as 300 during the late spring dwindled to as few as 50 by midsummer. More settlers arrived during the fall, but by the close of the year their number was still less than 200.[1] Daniel Boone expressed his faith in the area's future by bringing in his family through the Wilderness Road, but only a few other men followed his example that year.

Another complicating factor was the uncertainty about

land titles. Even if one assumed that independence would be declared and won, the problem remained. Would the new government take title to the relatively unsettled lands of the West and dispose of them as a national domain? Or would Virginia exercise the claims of an early royal charter that spoke grandly of boundaries that ran west to the sea and, according to one interpretation, gave the Old Dominion ownership of nearly half the continent? In March 1775, Judge Richard Henderson and his associates of the Transylvania Company negotiated the Treaty of Sycamore Shoals with the Cherokees. The company received Cherokee title to some 20,000,000 acres lying in the area roughly bounded by the Kentucky, Cumberland, and Ohio rivers, and it was obvious that Henderson's ambitions precluded subservience to Virginia authorities. Other companies were also interested in the region. Fertile land was the major attraction that lured men westward, but just which land titles would be valid in Kentucky?

With the area so remote, its inhabitants so few, and its political future so uncertain, it was inevitable that western interests would be neglected by easterners in favor of problems that to them seemed much more urgent. General George Washington knew the frontier from personal observation and extensive land speculation, but he was never able to spare from his limited resources enough men and supplies to mount an effective military effort in the Ohio Valley. Nor could Virginia, as she transformed herself from a colony into a state and labored to support the war for independence, devote much attention or effort to the land beyond the mountains that she might or might not decide to claim. Despite their anguished suspicions, the Kentuckians were not wantonly neglected by their eastern brethren; Kentucky simply did not have a high priority among the many pressing problems of the eastern governments.

News of the war trickled westward only slowly, but by word of mouth and an occasional newspaper or letter

Kentuckians gradually learned of the course of events back east. Weeks or even months after the fact they heard of Bunker Hill and the siege of Boston, of the unsuccessful invasion of Canada during the winter of 1775–1776 and the evacuation of Boston by the British in 1776. Some of them probably heard of relatives who went northward with Daniel Morgan and amazed the New Englanders with their use of the rifle. They were dismayed by Washington's near disasters on Long Island and Manhattan and his retreat across New Jersey as a dismal autumn turned into winter; they were encouraged by his victories at Trenton and Princeton that closed the 1776 campaign for the winter. While there were some Tories in Kentucky who found it difficult to renounce old allegiances, most Kentuckians approved of the Declaration of Independence. But could it be maintained? That question was still far from settled as 1776 drew to a close and the Continental army huddled in its winter quarters.

As long as the issue was in doubt, Kentucky could anticipate little help from either Virginia or the Continental government. Yet the Indian problem was becoming more critical. A great Indian conference held at Pittsburgh from September 26 to October 19, 1776, had produced a temporary truce along the Ohio frontier. The participating Indians pledged neutrality in the war, while the Americans promised not to move north of the Ohio River.[2] The agreement was frequently violated by both sides, however, and the Kentucky settlers lived in constant apprehension of raiding parties that made both hunting and farming hazardous occupations. Such British officials as General Guy Carleton opposed the use of Indians against the American frontiersmen, and the American invasion of Canada in 1775–1776 cut off the flow of British trade goods to the Great Lakes region. But even without British sponsorship and direction the Indian threat was serious enough that by the end of 1776 Kentucky's population was probably even less than it had been a year earlier.[3]

3

If the Kentucky settlements were to survive, they had to receive some assistance from the East. Gunpowder, for example, could not then be manufactured locally, and without an adequate supply the new settlements were doomed. There was also need for a governmental and military organization to make the most effective use of the limited resources that were available. Most of the Kentucky pioneers, although skilled woodsmen, were farmers rather than soldiers. Their primary concern had to be for their families and the crops upon which their survival depended. Afraid to venture far from the uncertain security of their cabins, they were forced into a defensive stance. Sooner or later they would probably succumb to the mounting pressures exerted against them. No one questioned the courage or forestlore of such leaders as Daniel Boone, James Harrod, and Benjamin Logan; they were indispensable in commanding their small stations and directing their small forces. But the situation in Kentucky demanded another type of leader—someone with a broader strategic vision, someone not tied to a single locality, someone who could marshal the scanty resources available in the West and wrestle some help from the governments in the East. Kentucky discovered such a leader in a twenty-three-year-old man named George Rogers Clark.

When he later described his career Clark wrote of 1775: "It was at this period that I first thought of paying some attention to the interest of the country." From then until the war in the West finally ended, well after its conclusion along the coast, Clark was the dominant military figure in Kentucky and the Illinois country. His story is much of the story of Kentucky during the American Revolution.

George Rogers Clark was born on November 19, 1752, in Albemarle County, Virginia, a short distance from the home of a nine-year-old youth named Thomas Jefferson. Both his father, John Clark, and his mother, Ann Rogers, were of predominantly British stock. Five years after the boy's birth the family moved to an inherited plantation in Caroline County. Little is known about Clark's childhood and youth. For a time he attended a school taught by Donald Robertson; here James Madison was one of Clark's fellow students. The boy learned something of mathematics, for he later qualified as a surveyor, and his interests as an adult reflected a knowledge of and a liking for geography and history. Clark enjoyed reading, and he developed a vigorous prose style, marred somewhat by erratic spelling and eccentric punctuation. The family was moderately prosperous, but John Clark believed in instilling discipline and a sense of responsibility into his nine children. When George was fifteen, his father's account book credited the boy with the income from his tobacco crop but debited him for the expense of his clothing and other personal items. The following year the boy sold his corn and tobacco for thirty pounds.

In 1772, by then a tall, slender, yet powerful young man with reddish hair and a fair complexion, Clark made his first western trip. The Reverend David Jones, describing his western experiences that year, remarked that traveling with him was "a certain young gentleman from Virginia who is inclined to make a tour in this new world."[4] Their small party went down the Ohio as far as the mouth of the Great Kanawha River, explored that area, then returned home through the mountains. Impressed by the region, Clark returned two months later, accompanied by his father, a friend, and two slaves. He claimed good bottom land some distance below Wheeling, cleared a portion of it and planted corn, and surveyed for other settlers who were moving into that region. During the next two years Clark shuttled back and forth between his parental home and his own holding. In 1773 he explored farther to the west with a party headed for Kentucky, a land that increasingly fascinated Clark.

This idyllic life was interrupted by Lord Dunmore's War, which erupted in the Fort Pitt region in 1774. Smouldering troubles were stirred into flame by a series of white atrocities and Indian retaliations, and on June 10 Dunmore, the last royal governor of Virginia, called out a portion of the colony's militia. Although the records are incomplete, Clark had apparently been commissioned a "Captain of Militia of Pittsburg and Its Dependencies" during the spring. He accompanied the column led by Lord Dunmore and thus missed the Battle of Point Pleasant, where Colonel Andrew Lewis commanded. Although Clark saw little if any actual fighting, the campaign was pivotal in his career. He discovered that he possessed the gift of command; he acquired invaluable knowledge about the strengths and weaknesses of militia; he learned a great deal about the Indian way of thinking and fighting; and he met a number of men with whom he would be associated during the next several years. Clark also acquired some knowledge of military organization and an appreciation of its value in conducting a wilderness campaign.

A number of Clark's friends had explored in Kentucky by 1775, and he was attracted to that land by their tales of fertile soil, grassy meadows, and the towering forests that teemed with game of every kind. Even Richard Henderson despaired of doing justice to Kentucky's full glory: "A description of the country is a vain attempt, there being nothing else to compare with it, and therefore could be only known to those who visit it."[5] Clark entered central Kentucky for the first time in 1775 as a surveyor for the Ohio Company. His salary was eighty pounds per year, but he could also take up lands for himself, a privilege that he quickly exercised.

He assisted Colonel Hancock Lee in laying out the location for Leesburg near the future site of Frankfort; it would have fifty inhabitants by Christmas, Clark declared erroneously. That was the spot where he intended to live, he wrote a brother in July: "A richer and more beautiful country than this, I believe has never been seen in America yet." He would not advise their father about moving to Kentucky, "but I am convinced that if he once sees ye country, he never will rest until he gets in it to live."⁶

As a landholder, Clark was disturbed by the disputes over ownership that might jeopardize his titles. The most immediate danger was Judge Henderson, who had come to Kentucky earlier in the year to push the claims of the Transylvania Company. Clark opposed Henderson's ambitions, and he was delighted to see that the judge had forfeited much support by an ill-advised increase in land prices. A decisive factor in the ownership controversy would be the attitude of Virginia, and Clark decided to return east to ascertain what that attitude would be.

He left Kentucky in the fall of 1775 and returned the following spring. As he sounded opinions, Clark found a fluid situation with the ultimate decision uncertain. He saw the possibility of influencing the outcome by exerting pressure on the Virginia government. "I immediately fixed on my plans," Clark recalled, "that of assembling the people, get them to Elect deputies and send them to the Assembly of Virginia and treat with them respecting the Cuntrey. If valuable conditions was procured, to declare ourselves citizens of the State, otherways, establish an independent government, and, by giving away great part of the lands and disposing of the remainder otherways, we could not only gain great numbers of inhabitants, but in good measure protect them."⁷

Soon after his arrival at Harrodsburg, Clark proposed holding a general meeting there on June 6. James Harrod, a friend from Dunmore's War, had also considered calling such a gathering but with a significant difference: Harrod wanted to elect delegates to represent Kentucky in the Virginia General Assembly; Clark favored representatives who would negotiate the future status of Kentucky with the Virginia government.⁸ Clark's call for the meeting was deliberately vague to avoid the formation of factions and to present an air of mystery that would help ensure a large turnout.

For some unexplained reason, Clark was delayed and

did not reach Harrodsburg on the appointed day until late evening. In his absence the confused settlers had elected Clark and John Gabriel Jones, a young lawyer, as delegates to the General Assembly. Armed with appropriate petitions, they were to seek the creation of a new county in the West. In their bid for support the petitioners hinted of the aid that such an organization would allow them to give to the "laudable cause of American Freedom." It was foolish for "such a respectable body of prime riflemen to remain in a state of neutrality" while war was being waged in the East.[9] In the event, however, the cries for aid came from the western settlements, not from the seaboard.

The two young delegates started their long overland journey a few days later, hoping to arrive in eastern Virginia before adjournment of the convention that was transforming the colony into a commonwealth. Their dangerous trip was slowed when they suffered severely from "scald feet," a painful inflammation caused by prolonged friction between wet skin and wet leather. Several of the settlements along the way had been abandoned under the threat of Indian raids, but the travelers made the trip safely. When they arrived in Williamsburg in early November they were disappointed to learn that the convention had adjourned and the General Assembly would not meet until the following October, but Clark and Jones agreed to linger until they could present their case. Jones returned to the Holston River settlements of North Carolina while Clark remained in eastern Virginia.

Clark soon visited Governor Patrick Henry at his Hanover County home where the governor was recovering from an illness. Henry listened sympathetically to Clark's recital of the problems and needs of the westerners, and he agreed that a supply of gunpowder was the most urgently needed commodity. Obtaining a favorable letter from the governor, Clark appeared before the Executive

Council and requested 500 pounds of powder for the defense of Kentucky. His argument that the western settlements could not survive without it was accepted by the councilors, but they feared to give the powder to an area that might not be a part of the state. Instead, they offered to lend 500 pounds of powder to their "Friends in Distress," provided that Clark would arrange for its delivery and be personally responsible for its repayment if the Assembly did not extend jurisdiction over the region. They regretted that they could do no more to help "a detached people . . . not yet united to the state of Virginia."[10]

He could not accept the powder on such terms, Clark declared, and he warned that "the people might be destroyed for want of this small supply." Clark realized that more was at stake than delivery of the desperately needed gunpowder. If the Virginia government accepted even partially the responsibility of defending Kentucky, it would be extending de facto recognition of its jurisdiction over that area. That was the goal toward which the young man was by then working, and as he left the council he had already decided upon his next step.

"I wrote to the Council and enclosed the order," he related, "informing them that I had weighed the matter and found that it was out of my power to convey these stores, at my own expense, such a distance through an enemy's country; that I was sorry to find that we should have to seek protection elsewhere, which I did not doubt of getting; that if a country was not worth protecting, it was not worth claiming." Clark was a master psychologist, and his threat had the effect for which he had hoped. The Council reconsidered, sent for Clark, and informed him on August 23, 1776, that the 500 pounds of powder would be sent to Fort Pitt, to be "delivered to the said George Rogers Clark, or his order, for the use of the said inhabitants of Kentucki."[11] Pleased with both the gift of the powder and the implied recognition of Virginia's claims, Clark wrote to Kentucky to arrange for a party to pick up the powder as quickly as possible and convey it to the Kentucky forts.

Legal recognition of Virginia's claim to Kentucky was still needed, so Clark and Jones remained in Virginia to work for that goal at the fall session of the General Assembly. Although they were refused seats as delegates, they received a sympathetic hearing, and such friendly members as Thomas Jefferson fought valiantly to get Kentucky created as a county with its own local government. The Indiana Company protested the state's claim to the western lands, and Judge Henderson lobbied hard to protect the fading prospects of the Transylvania Company. He was aided by Colonel Arthur Campbell, lieutenant of Fincastle County, who would lose much of the area under his jurisdiction if the organization was accomplished. Clark argued convincingly that the Kentucky settlements were essential for the protection of the Virginia frontier, and after numerous delays Kentucky County was finally created in early December of 1776. This action, which has been called "the political birth of Kentucky," was to earn for Clark the sobriquet "Founder of the Commonwealth."[12]

As the elated Kentucky delegates prepared to return to the settlements they had left so many months earlier, they were appalled to learn that the precious gunpowder was still at Pittsburgh. Although they did not know why, Clark's letter had never reached Kentucky. Quickly changing their plans, Clark and Jones hastened to Fort Pitt where they claimed the powder and recruited a small crew to help carry the kegs down the Ohio. Clark was convinced that the Indians were preparing for a general war in 1777, and he suspected that many of the red men who lounged around the fort were spies. In case they might try to intercept his boat, Clark and his party slipped away from the settlement and labored to outdistance any pursuers. As they neared Limestone Creek on the Kentucky shore, Clark decided that they were about to be overtaken. Unwilling to run the risk of losing his cargo, he buried the powder in several spots and continued downstream for a few miles before abandoning the boat.

Clark, Jones, and their small crew started overland for Harrodsburg, where they expected to find a large enough party to recover the powder safely. On the way they met four men who were exploring land in that area. Clark and two companions pushed on for the settlement; Jones and the rest were to wait for their return. But soon after Clark's departure John Todd and a few men arrived in the neighborhood where Jones and his party were camped. After some discussion ten of the men started for the Ohio River to secure the powder. On Christmas Day they were defeated by a band of Indians who killed Lawyer Jones and two other men. One of the three whites captured was Joseph Rogers, a cousin of Clark. A week later James Harrod and thirty riflemen recovered the powder and distributed it among the hard-pressed stations.

The powder was put to good use in 1777, for in that year the British government began to use the Indians against the settlements in the West as they had already done in some sectors of the eastern frontier. Lieutenant Governor Henry Hamilton had suggested from his Detroit headquarters that "Parties of Indians conducted by proper Leaders" be sent against the American frontier, and on June 16, 1777, he received a copy of an order sent to General Carleton by Lord Germain, the British secretary of state for American colonies. "It is the King's Command," the order read, "that you should direct Lieut. Governor Hamilton to assemble as many of the Indians of his District as he conveniently can, and placing proper persons at their Head. . . . to conduct their Parties, and restrain them from committing violence on the well affected and inoffensive Inhabitants, employ them in making a Diversion and exciting an alarm upon the frontiers of Virginia and Pennsylvania." A month later Hamilton reported that fifteen war parties, averaging nineteen warriors and two whites each, had already left Detroit.[13]

The most devastating Indian raids that Kentucky had ever endured began months before the official British sanction was finally received. The laconic entries in a diary Clark kept during this period give some idea of the pressure under which the Harrodsburg settlers lived. "Nothing remarkable done" disposed of February, but the Indians appeared with the first hints of spring.

March 6. Thomas Shores & Wm. Ray killed at the Shawnee Spring.

March 7. The Indians attempted to cut off from the fort a small party of our men. A skirmish ensued. We had 4 men wounded and some cattle killed. We killed and scalped one Indian, and wounded several.

18. A small party of Indians killed and scalped Hugh Wilson about ½ mile from the fort, near night, & escaped.

19. Archibald McNeal died of his wounds recd. 7th inst.

28. A large party of Inds attacked the stragglers about the fort; killed and scalped Garret Pandergreet; killed, or took prisoner, Peter Flin.

Such small actions were a continual drain upon the limited manpower and slender resources of the stations, and scores of the pioneers fled through Cumberland Gap to safer areas. As the number of riflemen dwindled, several of the smaller stations were abandoned and the survivors concentrated at Boonesborough, Harrodsburg, and Logan's Station (Saint Asaph's). According to one count, Kentucky had only 121 fighting men by the end of the year—84 at Harrodsburg, 22 at Boonesborough, 15 at Logan's Station. A more exact census taken at Harrodsburg in September counted a total population of 198, including 24 women, 58 white children under ten years of age, 12 white children over ten, and 19 slaves, of whom 7 were children under ten. With 4 white men judged unfit for service, there were 81 riflemen between the fort and extinction.[14]

Some of the 1777 raids were on a larger scale than the Kentuckians had previously endured. Shawnee chief

Blackfish attacked Harrodsburg in March; while he failed to take it, he delayed preparations for corn planting. Boone's fort was hit in mid-April, Logan's on May 20, Boone's again on July 4. From March until August the Kentuckians were under threat of almost constant attack. Food was scarce, for hunting was dangerous and few crops could be planted and harvested, even when riflemen tried to guard the fields against surprise attacks. Living conditions in the cramped forts became increasingly difficult. The invaluable livestock shared the limited space, and water supplies became contaminated. Disease took a toll almost as deadly as the enemy outside the stockades. Yet life continued, and there were occasional moments of mirth and enjoyment. On April 19 James Barry married the Widow Wilson, whose husband had been killed by the Indians six weeks earlier, and on July 9 Clark's diary recorded that "Lieutenant Linn married—great merriment."

By the summer of 1777 George Rogers Clark carried some official responsibility for the safety of the Kentucky settlements. When the new county's government was organized, he was commissioned major in the militia. Since none of his superiors was in Kentucky, Clark was the ranking officer in that huge county. Among his subordinates were Captains Daniel Boone, James Harrod, Benjamin Logan, and John Todd. Clark's headquarters were at Harrodsburg, but he visited the other posts as often as possible. He realized that the most effective use of resources would come from concentrating the total population at one spot, but the people's dependence on hunting and their reluctance to leave their homes made such a strategy impossible.

Governor Henry, aware of the plight of his western constituents, ordered militia from some of the less exposed counties to Kentucky to help hold it or to "escort all the people with their effects to the nearest point of safety. . . ."[15] In late August, Colonel John Bowman reached Logan's Station with a hundred men, and other reinforcements arrived later. They could not remain long, but their presence eased the immediate danger, and the coming of fall usually marked a decrease in Indian raids. This relatively peaceful interlude allowed Clark to make another trip to eastern Virginia to seek support for a daring and ambitious plan that he believed would save the Kentucky settlements.

Clark had labored incessantly to keep the settlements alive, but he feared that the effort would prove futile if their resources continued to be depleted through attrition. If the pioneers were not killed or did not flee to safer areas, they might in despair make "their peace with Detroit and suffer themselves and their families to be carried off." When his duties permitted time for reflection, Clark pondered the crisis that confronted his people. "This led me to a long train of thinking," he said, "the result of which was to lay aside every private view and engage seriously in the war and have the interest and welfare of the public my only view, . . . to persue [*sic*] what I conceived to be the interest of the whole."

As Clark saw the situation, the destruction of the Kentucky forts would be followed by massive raids against the more easterly frontier. The tribes would be so protected by distance that eastern armies would be unable to reach them. The survival of Kentucky, therefore, was vital for those living in the East, and they should be willing to supply the assistance necessary for the security of the western country. Kentucky's survival could only be assured, Clark concluded, by taking the offensive and carrying the war into the enemy's territory. Forces based in Kentucky would be able to reach most of the western Indians who were assisting the British. His plan was to drive the British out of their posts north of the Ohio and to defeat or neutralize their Indian allies in that region.

Clark was always a believer in gathering as much information as possible before embarking upon an undertaking, and in April 1777 he sent Benjamin Linn and Samuel Moore into the Illinois country to see what they could discover there. They went first to Spanish-held Saint Louis, where they posed as hunters who needed to trade beaver pelts for supplies. Then they crossed the Mississippi River and investigated Kaskaskia and some of the other French communities. Forced to flee when authorities became suspicious, they reported back to Clark in June. He also acquired information from such Americans as Thomas Bentley and David Murray, who had lived in the French towns for several years.

As he pieced together his intelligence, Clark concluded that the British in the Illinois country were diligent in performing their duties but "had but little expectation of a visit from us. . . ." Most of the Indians had joined the British, but many of the French inhabitants were either neutral or inclined to favor the Americans. While Clark was already dreaming of capturing Detroit—and then perhaps eliminating the British from the lower Mississippi region—his first goal was Kaskaskia, a town of some 1,000 inhabitants. Its capture would cut off one of Detroit's sources of supply, give control of important river communications, neutralize the Indian danger, and help maintain the tenuous supply routes to the Spanish settlements. But Kentucky County could not give him either permission to undertake the invasion or the resources that might achieve success; Clark had to seek both authorization and assistance from the Virginia government.

When Clark left Kentucky on October 1, 1777, many of his friends thought that he was abandoning the western lands, for he had kept silent about his plans. His original party of twenty-two men was slowed by the addition of men, women, and children who sought the protection of a large, well-armed group. Their accretion testified to the seriousness of the crisis in the West; unless the exodus could be stemmed, the Kentucky settlements would soon be lost.

Clark visited one full day with his parents and then pushed on to Williamsburg, where he arrived on November 5. During the next few days as he sought to ascertain public opinion and the attitudes of those in power, the young major settled his militia accounts with the state auditors, bought a lottery ticket, attended church, and purchased cloth and buttons for a new jacket. Evidently deciding that the time was not propitious for revealing his plans, Clark returned to Caroline County for a longer visit with his family.

He was encouraged by the news of the war in the East. The surrender of General John Burgoyne at Saratoga in October had been the greatest American victory of the conflict; it had done much to lift morale throughout the states. The struggle, however, was far from being over. General Washington had lost Philadelphia to General William Howe, and the Continental soldiers at Valley Forge were enduring one of their most difficult winters of the war. There were hints that the British might transfer their main military effort to the southern states. If they did so, Virginia was almost certain to become more directly involved in military action than she had previously been. Her economy was already strained by the contributions she had made to the northern campaigns, and serious inflation was eroding the value of paper currency at a terrifying rate.

Clark arrived back in Williamsburg on December 10 and communicated his proposal to the governor the same day. Henry was attracted to the plan, but he was aware of its danger and of the need for secrecy if it was to have any chance of success. Several questions troubled him. Would Virginia retain any of the land beyond the Ohio, or would it become part of a national domain? Would an expedition into that area rouse the Indians to even greater hostility? Would France accept the seizure of a region that contained many French residents? What would be the attitude of Spain? Was success possible with the limited resources available? Could Clark do the job?

Clark was a persuasive advocate, and as he explained his scheme to the governor and some of his closest advisors, he allayed their doubts. His listeners were impressed by the detail in which Clark had thought out his plan, and he convinced them that he might succeed. Thomas Jefferson, George Mason, and George Wythe were among those consulted. They promised to seek liberal land grants for those who participated in the enterprise. In a letter to Clark they suggested that a private might hope to receive 300 acres, with others rewarded in proportion to their ranks.[16]

Legislative approval was necessary, but the full plan was concealed to preserve secrecy. The Council apparently received the governor's recommendations on January 2, 1778. It approved Henry's drafted instructions, authorized the expenditure of £ 1,200 in depreciated currency, and gave the command to Clark. The General Assembly passed a vaguely worded act that authorized the governor and council to mount an expedition "to march against and attack any of our western enemies."[17] Few legislators knew what was being planned; it was generally assumed that the troops were to be used for the defense of Kentucky. George Rogers Clark, now promoted to lieutenant colonel in the Virginia army, would have agreed with that assumption; but he was preparing to defend Kentucky by taking the offensive against her most dangerous foes.

Governor Henry gave Colonel Clark two sets of instructions. The public set ordered him to enlist seven companies of fifty men each from any county in the commonwealth. "They are to proceed to Kentucky, and there obey such orders and directions as you shall give them, for three months after their arrival at that place. . . ." Henry's secret instructions left Clark with wide discretion, and a later letter gave him authority to look beyond the capture of Kaskaskia. "Proceed as you find the Interest of your Country directs, when you get to the place you are going to," Henry wrote. "What I have in View is that your operations should not be confined to the Fort & the Settlement mention'd in your secret Instructions but that you proceed to the Enemy's Settlements above or across [i.e., to Detroit or Vincennes], as you may find it proper."[18]

Within the next few weeks Clark selected his chief officers and started them upon the vital task of recruiting. Joseph Bowman, who became the second-in-command, was to raise a company in Fauquier County while Leonard Helm recruited in Frederick. The other captains were John M. Montgomery (one of the Long Hunters who had visited Kentucky in 1771–1772) and William Harrod, who, along with his brother, James, had become acquainted with Clark during Dunmore's campaign. Troops were also to be raised in the Holston settlements and marched overland to meet those coming down the Ohio. By early spring of 1778 George Rogers Clark expected to be ready to begin his war.

2

THE ILLINOIS
CAMPAIGN, 1778

CLARK HAD ESTIMATED that he could accomplish his
objectives with 500 men, and he had anticipated little
difficulty in securing the 350 authorized by the state
authorities. But he encountered disappointments from
the outset. Recruiters for the Continental army and for
state troops competed with Clark's officers, and, despite
the authority granted in his instructions, Governor Henry
was soon complaining that Clark was recruiting too far
east. The men who joined him, Henry warned, would not
be exempt from the state draft.[1] An ancient boundary
dispute between Pennsylvania and Virginia had become
so bitter that few Pennsylvanians would assist what they
judged to be a Virginia enterprise. And since the Holston
settlers were more concerned with the Cherokees and
other tribes to the south than they were with Indians who
lived across the Ohio River, the harvest of volunteers was
also thin from this source. The Kentucky forts were so
undermanned and in such peril that few men could be
spared from them.

The intended departure from Redstone was delayed
repeatedly to allow time for more men to appear, but in
May, Clark decided that he could wait no longer. He
started down the Monongahela to the Forks of the Ohio

with some 150 men and a few civilian families that accompanied the troops for safety against Indian attacks. Supplies were picked up at Pittsburgh and Wheeling, but they were not met by any large number of additional riflemen. The party was large enough to discourage small bands of Indians, and the voyage was made safely. When they reached the mouth of the Great Kanawha, the commander of Fort Randolph, who had beaten off an attack by 250 Indians the day before, sought Clark's assistance in pursuing the enemy. Clark could not spare the time, and his little flotilla continued downstream.

Discouraging news greeted Clark when he halted at the mouth of the Kentucky River to unload some salt kettles that the Kentucky settlers needed badly. Instead of the 200 men expected from the Holston settlements, he would get a few dozen at the most. Clark could not realistically count on having more than 175 men. The news, he said, "made me as desperate as I was before determined." He realized that some of his troops would be appalled by the prospect of fighting far from home against a foe who outnumbered them several times over and who directed an even more numerous force of Indians. But Clark refused to give up. "I knew our case was desperate," he later admitted, "but the more I reflected on my weakness, the more I was pleased with the enterprise."

Uncertain of the soldiers' reaction when they finally learned their destination and realized how few they numbered, Clark decided to make his base and training camp on Corn Island, near the Falls of the Ohio and the future site of Louisville. They reached the island on May 27, 1778, and both soldiers and civilians were put to work immediately on constructing a base. Blockhouses and a stockade fence were thrown up for protection, cabins and storehouses were built, and a few acres were quickly cleared for planting late crops. The officers began to drill the men and to instill some semblance of discipline into them. As Clark later wrote a friend, "You already know the situation in which you left me at the Falls and the kind of people with whom I had to deal; but after I had knocked down some and punished and imprisoned others, they became the best people that can be imagined."[2] Those few who appeared unable to stand up to the rigors of the projected campaign Clark would leave behind as the garrison for the fort.

John Bowman brought in some Kentuckians from the interior forts, but Clark decided reluctantly that most of them would have to return home to help protect their settlements, which were themselves in desperate need of men. The Kentucky stations had received a jolting blow in February when Indians had captured Daniel Boone near Blue Licks; in order to save their lives, he had persuaded twenty-seven other saltmakers to surrender. Kentucky could ill afford such a loss, and Clark kept only a score of the Kentuckians who had volunteered their services. Among those who stayed was Simon Kenton, the peerless scout. Although many of Clark's men later became identified with the state, few of them could claim to be Kentuckians in 1778.

The time finally came for Clark to inform the men of his plans. Most of his officers were enthusiastic when Clark explained his scheme, although a few wondered if they were strong enough to attain his objectives. The men debated the plan at length with considerable apprehension being voiced, but they agreed at last to accept the officers' decision. Much of the dissatisfaction was centered in Captain Dillard's A Company. The boats were guarded to prevent desertion, but some of the men had discovered while swimming in the river that at one point it could be waded from the island to the Kentucky shore. During the night a Lieutenant Hutchings and much of the company slipped across the river and fled to escape George Rogers Clark's madness. When their loss was discovered, Clark sent horsemen in pursuit. Some of the men were captured and returned, but the rest escaped. They received a coward's reception, however, when they reached the settlements; some were not even allowed to enter the forts for some time.[3]

Clark's preparations were nearing completion, and the longer he delayed, the greater was the danger that his intentions might become known to the enemy. On June 24, 1778, with approximately 175 men Clark left Corn Island and its small garrison and few civilians. They pulled their boats upstream nearly a mile to get into the right channel for shooting the rapids. An eclipse of the sun as they departed may have alarmed some of the more superstitious among the soldiers; it did not daunt their leader, who had full confidence in their success. Since the British were keeping close watch on the river traffic at the junction of the Ohio and Mississippi rivers, Clark decided to stop short of that point and march overland to Kaskaskia. To keep ahead of any news of their coming, he ordered the oars double-manned, and the men ran the boats day and night until they reached the mouth of the Tennessee River, where they made a landing to complete their preparations for the overland march.

Shortly after their arrival they captured a small party of hunters, all of British nationality, who had left Kaskaskia only eight days earlier. When the mission was explained the hunters willingly took an oath of allegiance and asked permission to join the expedition. Clark allowed them to do so after some close questioning about the Illinois country and its residents; he had received no news from the Illinois towns since the return of his spies the previous year. John Saunders, who said he knew the region especially well, became the column's guide. The hunters told Clark that the fort at Kaskaskia was in good repair and the garrison alert; unless taken by surprise the French residents would probably give a good account of themselves, for they had "a most horrid idea of the barbarity of the rebels, especially of the Virginians. . . ."

"But no part of their information pleased me more," Clark wrote, "than that of the inhabitants viewing us as more savage than their neighbors, the Indians. I was determined to improve this, if I was fortunate enough to get them in my possession, as I conceived the greater the shock I could give them at first, the more sensibly they would feel my lenity, and become more valuable friends. This I conceived to be agreeable to human nature as I observed it in many instances."

They concealed the boats near abandoned Fort Massac, a few miles below the mouth of the Tennessee, and on the morning of June 29 started the 120-mile march across country.[4] Limited to what they could carry on their backs, they moved in single file to reduce the risk of some Indian scout discovering their trail. They had no uniforms as such. Most of the men were dressed in typical frontier-style hunting shirts that reached nearly to the knee, wide belts, leggings, moccasins, and droopy felt hats. In addition to his long rifle, each man carried a powderhorn, a hunting knife, and a tomahawk; his hunting pouch or a fold in his shirt carried whatever other items he considered essential.

The column moved swiftly until the third day, when Saunders lost his way. Aware of the precarious predicament in which they could find themselves, and suspicious of betrayal, Clark became enraged. He gave Saunders until sundown to find the hunters' trail leading to Kaskaskia; if the guide failed to find it, he would be executed. His memory sharpened by that incentive, Saunders was able to recover his sense of direction and get the expedition back on the proper trail before the deadline. Despite his danger, he became a devoted friend and follower of Clark. The scanty supply of food was exhausted by the end of the fourth day, and neither time nor security permitted hunting. During the last two days of their march the men lived on such wild berries as they could snatch on the way and by tightening their belts. But morale remained high.

On the evening of July 4 the weary men occupied a farmhouse on the eastern bank of the Kaskaskia River, less than a mile from the town. Clark learned that there had been an alarm over a possible attack several days earlier, but the fear had subsided. Most of the Indians who had been in the neighborhood had departed, and the townspeople had no hint that the Americans were near. Boats were found, and in two hours Clark's command was across the river. As the men moved silently toward the town, sounds of merriment indicated that they had achieved total surprise. The little army was quickly divided. Clark led one detachment toward the fort while the remaining men took up stations in the town, a sizable community of well-built houses and a population of nearly 500 whites and an equal number of blacks.

Clark's detachment broke into the fort without meeting any opposition and secured it within minutes. Governor Phillip Rocheblave and his wife were found in bed. His papers included much recent correspondence with Lieutenant Governor Hamilton at Detroit; they provided Clark with badly needed information about the enemy's resources. One early Kentucky historian contended that Madame Rocheblave took advantage of Clark's chivalry and either destroyed or concealed in her baggage some of the more important documents. Her ability to do so was regrettable, "but better, ten thousand times better, were it so, than that the ancient fame of the sons of Virginia should have been tarnished by insult to a female."[5]

When the fort was secured, the victors shouted as a signal for the other detachments to subdue the town. French-speaking American troops raced through the streets, calling out to the terrified citizens that the fort had been captured and that anyone who ventured into the streets would be shot. Details covered each road leading from the town to prevent word of the seizure from reaching other communities. The French were warned that anyone attempting to leave the town would be executed on the spot, and they were ordered to turn in their arms. The orders were obeyed. "I don't suppose greater silence ever reigned among the inhabitants of a place than did at this," Clark reported. At his orders, the troops kept up a barrage of noise throughout the remainder of the night, and occasionally an inhabitant was escorted by savage-looking riflemen to Clark for questioning. Few Frenchmen could have slept during the latter part of that terrifying night.

The nocturnal interviews revealed that many of the French were more sympathetic to the Americans than to the British cause. As stories poured from eager lips, Clark began to suspect that some of his informants were trying to win favor and settle old grudges by discrediting certain of their neighbors. A particular target was Gabriel Cerré, the town's most prominent merchant, who was then in Saint Louis preparing for a lengthy journey to Canada. To secure his return, Clark placed a guard over his home and stores, allowing word of this action to be carried across the river. With the most urgent tasks completed, some of the Americans were able to eat and sleep, while the Kaskaskians cowered in their homes, terrified of what the morrow might bring.

On the morning of July 5 Clark continued the psychological warfare he had plotted against the French inhabitants, whose support was essential if he was to hold the region. After breakfast some of his men were sent to reinforce the guards on the roads. Those who remained in town were ordered to ignore its residents. When the French were allowed on the streets, they were met by studied indifference. Their worst fears appeared realized when several of their militia officers were seized and placed in irons without any explanation being offered. Gallic imagination ran unchecked as the Americans continued their silence.

At last, urged on by a sense of desperation, a delegation of several elderly leaders led by Father Pierre Gibault, the town priest, obtained an audience with the American commander. Their apprehensions were increased when they faced Clark and his officers—a group of dirty, unshaven, half-naked savages. It was some moments before they rallied sufficiently to state their plea. They assumed that they were to be separated, perhaps never to meet again in this world, and they were resigned to that fate. But would it be allowed for them to meet in their church to pray together and to say their farewells? They could go to their church if they wished, Clark replied curtly, but no one was to leave the town. When the delegates sought to continue the conversation, Clark cut them off abruptly; he had no time then to talk with them. His qualification was, of course, designed to bring them back later for another attempt.

As the townspeople crowded into the church, Clark gave strict orders that no soldier was to enter the empty houses. After a time, as he had anticipated, Clark was again approached by the priest and some of the town's leaders. When they had thanked him for his indulgence, they ventured to raise some other points concerning their situation. They were reconciled to the loss of their property that would be left behind as they went into exile, but could the women and children take some clothing and provisions with them? And would it be possible for families to remain together when the exodus began? They had little knowledge of the American Revolution, the Frenchmen explained in an effort to secure understanding of their position; they had simply followed the orders of their commandants, who had been pro-British. Some of the people had been as much pro-American as they had dared to be.

Clark was delighted with the success of his approach. "This was the point I wished to bring them to," he wrote later. He interrupted their pleadings to ask if the French thought that they were dealing with savages. "Did they suppose that we meant to strip the women and children, and take the bread out of their mouths? or that we would condescend to make war on the women and children, or the church?" He was astounded that they should hold any such thoughts. He and his men had come to prevent the Indians from shedding innocent blood, not to plunder.

Then Clark revealed some news that visibly aroused old loyalties; the king of France had allied his country with the United States, and there was a possibility that the war would soon be over.

They were free, Clark continued, to go with either side without endangering their private property or having families broken up. All religions were protected in his country, and he would punish any insult to their church. He was convinced that they had been misled by false statements from some of their leaders, and for this reason he was willing to forget the past. They could resume normal lives. Their leaders who had been arrested would be released at once, and only Cerré's property would remain under guard.

When the delegates attempted to apologize for what Clark had thought were their harsh opinions of Americans, he gently halted their explanations. "I informed them I knew that they were taught to believe that we were little better than barbarians, but that we would say no more on the subject; that I wished them to go and relieve the anxiety of the inhabitants." Within minutes the mood of the town changed from dejection to joy. As the bell pealed, the church was again crowded with happy people who returned thanks for their deliverance, and Americans on the streets were greeted like old friends.

Although the Americans had captured the largest of the Illinois towns, much remained to be done. Cahokia, some fifty miles north, was reported to have a population of 300 whites and 80 blacks, and a large concentration of Indians was said to be in that vicinity. Prairie du Rocher, about fifteen miles north of Kaskaskia, contained 100 whites and 80 blacks, while nearby Saint Phillips was even smaller. Most important was Vincennes to the east. Its population was nearly as large as that of Kaskaskia, and it occupied a position of strategic importance. In American hands it could pose a threat to the tribes that were most dangerous to the Kentucky settlements, and it was a stepping stone toward the conquest of Detroit, Clark's first great objective.

Even as Clark applied his knowledge of psychology to the residents of Kaskaskia, he moved quickly and decisively to gain control of the other towns. Simon Kenton and two other scouts were sent to Vincennes to spy out the situation there. Captain Joseph Bowman mounted thirty men on horses obtained from the French and set out for Cahokia on the evening of July 5. He was accompanied by a few of the French, who proved most helpful in convincing other Frenchmen of the Americans' goodwill. Bowman and his cavalry had possession of Prairie du Rocher before its inhabitants realized they were being invaded; they readily agreed to whatever was demanded of them. Saint Phillips was occupied in the dead of night, and, as Bowman said, the inhabitants "seemed scared almost out of their wits as it was impossible that they could know my strength."[6]

Pushing himself and his men relentlessly, Bowman hurried on to Cahokia, where he demanded surrender of the astounded commander. The Frenchman had no choice but to comply, but he balked at taking the oath of allegiance immediately, despite the recommendations of the Kaskaskians who had accompanied Bowman on his hectic ride. The Americans spent an uneasy night in a well-fortified stone house, for Bowman had heard that a local man planned to overwhelm the Americans with 150 Indian warriors. Bowman arrested the suspect at once and no attack came, but he and his men endured their third consecutive sleepless night.

By ten o'clock the next morning 105 citizens had taken the oath, and in less than ten days the number had increased to 300, including those in the smaller towns that had been taken. Bowman was left in command of the detachment stationed at Cahokia, and the fort that he had taken was renamed in his honor. He set his men to work at once repairing the fortifications. The great majority of the inhabitants proved cooperative, but when a man named Denny was discovered to have corresponded with Hamilton at Detroit, he was quickly and publicly punished as a warning to the rest. "He was tied to the tail of a cart, and driven through the town, receiving a lash at every door," Clark explained. "He was also branded in the hand for other misdemeanors. This was the first and the severest punishment inflicted by us on any of the inhabitants. It was necessary at this time to convince the people that we were capable of extremes either way, and that the good treatment we had heretofore shown was due to our principles of government."

Clark used the Cerré case to consolidate further his status with the French. When the merchant learned in Saint Louis that some of his debtors were attempting to besmirch his reputation, he sought a safe conduct before crossing the river to defend himself. But Clark was at his most adamant; no assurance would be given, but an innocent person would return anyway to clear himself of damaging allegations. As Clark had anticipated, Cerré soon arrived to deny that he had incited Indians against the American frontier or had actively assisted the British. He was a merchant who tried to get along with everyone, Cerré explained, and he charged that his detractors hoped to void their debts by ruining him.

Clark knew that the community was following the case with intense interest; it had become a test of his fairness and skill in handling the affairs of the Illinois country. Calling all parties together, Clark told them that he wanted to establish the truth of the charges so that Cerré could be found guilty or acquitted. Placing the burden of proof upon those who had brought the charges, Clark called upon them to press their claims. Their courage melted under Clark's scrutiny and in Cerré's presence, and no one dared press the case. Clark then reprimanded those responsible for malicious statements and congratulated Cerré upon his honorable acquittal. The grateful merchant asked permission to take the oath of allegiance, and in the future he performed invaluable services for Clark. "As simple as this may appear," Clark wrote of the affair, "it had great weight with the people and was of infinite service to us." The installation of civil courts with elected judges both relieved Clark of some judicial burdens and gave the citizens a taste of American political democracy.

Friendly relations were also soon established with the young Spanish commander at Saint Louis, Fernando de Leyba, whose headquarters were only a few miles distant from Cahokia. During the next several months Clark found an occasional opportunity to relax as well as to conduct business in the hospitable environs of Saint Louis. During his first visit, which lasted two days, Clark was greeted by an artillery salute, entertained at a formal dinner for thirty guests and at dances and late suppers each evening, and lodged in de Leyba's home. Tradition has it that George Rogers Clark fell in love with Terese, the sister of Don Fernando. If the story is true, their blighted romance provides one answer to the question of why Clark never married.[7]

Clark was soon able to extend his conquests by occupying Vincennes. Kenton and the other scouts had penetrated the town three consecutive nights by wrapping themselves in blankets and masquerading as Indians. They reported that there was no British garrison and that most hostile Indians appeared to have left that neighborhood. When Clark let it be known that he contemplated calling up more troops from the Ohio to take Vincennes, Father Gibault and some of the other leading citizens assured him that such reinforcements were not needed. They had heard that Edward Abbott, the British officer at Vincennes, had already returned to Detroit, and they were sure that they could persuade their compatriots to accept American occupation. The priest suggested that he and Dr. Jean B. LaFont make the attempt.

"This was perfectly agreeable to what I had been secretly aiming at for some days," Clark almost chortled, since there were no troops that he could have called to assist him. A few others, including one of Clark's men, accompanied the two chief delegates, although Father Pierre had been thoroughly briefed on how to deal with various contingencies. The envoys departed on July 14, armed with numerous letters to friends and relatives in Vincennes from the satisfied citizens of Kaskaskia. The mission was successful. A few dissidents fled, but most of the residents took the oath of allegiance promptly and cheerfully. A French officer of the militia was elected to head the military establishment, and he unfurled the American flag over the fort. The envoys, accompanied by some Vincennes citizens, returned to Kaskaskia about the first of August to report their success.

Since Vincennes was such an important point, Clark decided to send Captain Leonard Helm there to take command. Considerably older than most of the other officers, Helm was a solid, dependable, fun-loving man, very popular with his associates. He had considerable experience in dealing with the Indians, and he played an important role in Clark's efforts to neutralize the tribes in the Illinois country. The change of command at Vincennes had an obvious effect upon the Indians in that area, and Helm worked diligently to capitalize upon it.

The messages that Helm carried from Clark to the Indians were quite different from those they had been accustomed to hearing. "You Indians living on the Wabash!" Clark said in a typical address. "We are not come with design to take your lands from you. . . . We only desire to pass through your country to Detroit, to turn out your Father who is there; for your late Father, the King of France, is come to life, and will recover the country he lost to the English. . . . We desire you to leave a very wide path for us, as we are many in number and love to have room enough for our march; for, in swinging our arms as we walk, we may chance to hurt some of your young people with our swords."

Clark played heavily upon the Indian affection for the

French who had been among them in earlier years. The king of France "had joined the Big Knife, and was mad at [the Indians] for fighting for the English; ... [he] would advise them to make peace with the Americans as soon as they could, otherwise they might expect the land to be very bloody."

Among the Indian chiefs most impressed by this approach was a Piankeshaw known as "Tobacco's Son" or the "Grand Door to the Wabash" in tribute to his influence in that region. After receiving Clark's message and consulting with his advisors, the Grand Door told Helm that he had decided the Big Knives were in the right and the British had misled him. He would tell the Wabash tribes "to bloody the land no more for the English," and he declared proudly that he was "now a Big Knife." During the two years before his death he was a zealous friend of the Americans, and as he neared death he asked to be buried with his white friends. His wishes were honored with a military funeral at Cahokia.

Clark engaged directly in most of the Indian negotiations, for he was the one they viewed with awe. His typical approach was to offer a tribe two belts—one for peace, the other for war. He refused to beg them to select the peace belt, and he disdained to offer bribes to buy their support. (He lacked the necessary resources to do so had he wanted to.) Instead, if they chose war, he exhorted them to "fight like men, that the Big Knives may not be ashamed when they fight you—that the old women may not tell us that we only fought squaws." Theirs was the choice of peace or war. "This is the last speech you may ever expect from the Big Knives; the next thing will be the tomahawk. And you may expect, in four moons, to see your women and children given to the dogs to eat, while nations that have kept their words with me will flourish and grow like the willow trees on the river banks, under the care and nourishment of their father, the Big Knives."[8]

During the latter part of August a number of tribes came to Cahokia to meet with Clark and to consider their future position. Clark's force there was greatly outnumbered and his confident demeanor concealed a considerable degree of apprehension. His fears seemed realized when a group of Puans tried to seize him in his headquarters by seeking refuge there from a mock attack on the other side of a creek. But Clark was awake, the guard was alert, and the wet leggings of those who had waded the creek allowed quick identification. The chiefs were put in irons and during the next few days were not allowed to speak, as the council continued in an atmosphere of growing dread and apprehension on the part of the Indians.

To flaunt his disregard for their intentions, Clark continued to stay in a house outside the fort; the guards even appeared to have been withdrawn. In reality, he had 50 riflemen concealed in the house, and the rest of the garrison was kept on alert. As final proof of his confidence, Clark staged a dance for the townspeople that lasted most of a night.

When the grand council opened, Clark maintained an aloof attitude that rebuffed the Indians' overtures of friendship. He and his officers would not shake hands with them, he indicated, because peace had not been made; "It was time enough to give the hand when the heart could be given also." Then in a long oration he explained to the worried, attentive chiefs how the war had come about and how the United States had been formed. After years of colonial discontent, "at last the Great Spirit took pity on us and kindled a great council fire that never gave out, at a place called Philadelphia, struck down a post, and left a tomahawk by it, and went away. . . . Thus the war began, and the English were driven from one place to another until they got weak and hired you Red People to fight for them and help them." But, he continued, "the Great Spirit, getting angry at this, he caused your old Father the French King and other nations to join the Big Knife and fight with them all their enemies, so that the English is become like a deer in the woods."

They must decide between the white belt of peace and the red one of war, Clark declared. If they chose war, they would be free to join their English friends, where he hoped they would fight like brave warriors. If they chose peace, they must not thereafter listen again "to bad birds that will be flying through your land," or they would risk destruction. Then Clark adjourned the council and sent the chiefs off to deliberate among themselves.

When they returned the next day with impressive ceremony, the spokesman for the Indians confessed that "the Big Knife did not speak like any other people that they had ever heard." But they had concluded that the English had lied to them while the Big Knives had told the truth. The Indians had, therefore, selected the peace belt, and they would "cast the tomahawk into the river, where it could never be found again. . . ." They would cooperate with the Americans and would advise their friends to do the same. The meeting ended with such stately ceremony that Clark imagined it comparable to that attending the signing of the recent treaty with France.

Turning then to the chained Puan chiefs, Clark informed them haughtily that they were old women, "too mean to be killed by a Big Knife." As long as they remained, they would be treated as squaws. When these chiefs attempted to present a peace pipe, Clark smashed it with a sword, saying that the Big Knives did not treat with women. Other chiefs begged Clark to relent, but he remained firm until two young warriors came forward to offer themselves as sacrifices to atone for their tribe's guilt. "I always intended at last to be persuaded to grant these people peace," Clark admitted, "but this astounded me." There was a long silence as the crowd waited in suspense for his decision. Overcome by admiration for their courage, Clark praised the two warriors for proving that there were men among their nation. And because of them, he said, he granted peace and friendship to their people.

This concluded a rather typical Clark performance in Indian negotiations, and it shows the skill with which he played upon the imaginations, fears, and emotions of his adversaries. His diplomatic philosophy was best summed up in his statement that he "gave Harsh language to supply the want of Men; well knowing that it was a mistaken notion in many that soft speeches were best for Indians." Few frontier leaders of his generation could match Clark's success in treating with the Indians; during the five weeks he spent at Cahokia in 1778 he concluded treaties with at least ten tribes. Clark followed up his success by placing agents among the tribes to make sure that they were sincere in their protestations of peace; he was gratified to see that most of the Illinois tribes remained true to the pledges they made. A modern historian of the frontier concluded, "The great achievement of Clark's 1778 campaign was not the uncontested occupation of the Illinois, but his success in neutralizing so considerable a segment of the Indian military power upon which English strategy had depended."[9]

When he returned to Kaskaskia, Clark reflected that "it was now I saw my work was only begun. . . . my situation and weakness convinced me that more depended on my own behavior and conduct than all the troops that I had." The number of troops had become a serious problem, one made more acute by the need to garrison several towns. The men's original term of enlistment had neared its end soon after the capture of Kaskaskia, and a large number of them indicated a strong desire to return home. By extending his authority beyond its legal limit and exerting his utmost powers of persuasion, Clark had cajoled nearly 100 into reenlisting for eight months. The other 70 had been sent off on August 4 under command of William Linn, who was to discharge them at the Falls of the Ohio.

Captain Montgomery accompanied the party to carry official reports to Virginia and to escort Rocheblave to captivity in that state.

In order to disguise the weakness of his command, Clark wrote and spoke of the "Headquarters Western American Army, Falls of the Ohio, Illinois Detachment"; he made sure that some of the local citizens saw letters carrying that grandiose title. More troops could be called up if he needed them, but he graciously accepted a company or more of French volunteers who wanted to join his force. In fact, the American "army" was so small that Clark avoided all parades and other gatherings that would have assembled his soldiers at one place; he dared not reveal how weak was the force that he commanded. But he labored to instill in the troops something of his own spirit, and he drilled them hard to achieve the discipline upon which he insisted. Yet he realized the need for some occasional relaxation, and a Kaskaskia merchant made out a bill "to 20 Bottles Rum furnished Colo. George Roger Clark's Detachment for a refreshment after their taking possession of Illinois Country."[10]

Colonel Clark also faced difficult and persistent supply problems. He could expect little help from Virginia, and the Kentucky settlements could not spare much from their insufficient stores. Some foodstuffs could be obtained in the Illinois country when money was available to make the purchases, and a trickle of welcome goods came from the friendly Spanish authorities on the far bank of the Mississippi River. But Oliver Pollock, the New Orleans fiscal agent for both Virginia and the Continental Congress, did more than anyone else to help. Indefatigable in his efforts, Pollock overcame innumerable obstacles to keep Clark supplied with the goods he had to have. Pollock was critically handicapped by the failure of the state and Continental governments to honor the bills drawn on them by Clark and others operating in the West, and he was forced to pledge his own property and credit to maintain the flow of supplies. His subsequent bankruptcy was a tribute to the zeal with which he supported the American cause. Clark could not have maintained his position in Illinois as long as he did had it not been for Pollock's efforts.

As Clark received news from Kentucky and Virginia he realized more clearly the extent to which he was dependent upon his own resources. General Washington and Congress had planned a summer expedition against Detroit from a base at Pittsburgh. General Lachlan McIntosh was given a force several times the size of Clark's command, but he had been ineffective and the effort had been abandoned.[11]

Relieved of the pressure that McIntosh's expedition should have provided, the Shawnees raided Kentucky again. Daniel Boone had escaped from captivity in June and in an amazing feat of endurance covered 160 miles in four days to warn the settlers of the impending attack. When the Indians failed to appear, Boone's trustworthiness was questioned. The Indians finally appeared in September, some 400 of them under Chief Blackfish, assisted by the French-Canadian officer DeQuindre and several other whites. After a parley, the leaders of the Boonesborough fort agreed to renounce their allegiance to the United States and renew fealty to the British crown if the Indians would withdraw. But the besiegers did not carry out their part of the bargain, and all of their stratagems failed to take the fort.[12] After an unusually long siege of thirteen days, the Indians withdrew.

Boone's reputation then came under serious scrutiny. His apparent willingness to change sides and the alacrity with which he had surrendered the salt-making party at Blue Licks early in the year led to formal charges of treason. He answered all the charges to the satisfaction of the court and was acquitted, but the fact that Daniel Boone was even tried told much about the state of affairs

37

in Kentucky. In view of conditions there, Clark could expect little or no additional aid from the Kentucky settlements.

Clark's news of what was occurring in the East was delayed and often incomplete; it may have been well into 1779 before he got a clear idea of the events of the previous year. The news was not encouraging when it finally arrived, for the war appeared to have reached a sort of stalemate despite the French alliance. The British continued to hold New York, and they occasionally raided coastal towns. When General Henry Clinton, under orders to evacuate Philadelphia, decided to march much of his army overland to New York, he was attacked by Washington's army at Monmouth, New Jersey. General Charles Lee failed to carry out his orders, and Clinton was able to beat off the assault and make good his march into the city that the British were to hold for the remainder of the war. Toward the end of the year it became evident that the British were turning their major attention to the southern theater that had been relatively quiet.

With the outcome of the struggle still so uncertain, Clark could not expect substantial assistance from either Congress or Virginia. He had not even had a message from Governor Henry for nearly a year. Clark was isolated in the Illinois country with resources too limited to achieve the goals he longed to attain. Then he learned that his situation was even more serious than he had imagined; a British expedition from Detroit had retaken Vincennes.

3

THE VINCENNES CAMPAIGN

INCOMPLETE NEWS of the American invasion, sped northward by one Francis Maisonville who had been in the Illinois country when the American arrived, reached Detroit on August 6. The news came as both a shock and a disappointment to Lieutenant Governor Henry Hamilton, who had been marshaling resources for an attack on Fort Pitt. Simon Girty, among others, had been collecting information about the disposition of military forces in western Pennsylvania. Now Hamilton's attention would have to be turned elsewhere.

Hamilton came from a Scottish family with Irish holdings, and many of his kinsmen had been prominent in government and military service. His infantry regiment had been sent to America during the French and Indian War, and he had been wounded while serving in General James Wolfe's command. During a visit to some of the American colonies, Hamilton had described their inhabitants as "naive, simple, kindly and uncorrupted"—an opinion he later changed. Appointed lieutenant governor in charge of the Detroit district in April 1775, he arrived at his new post on November 7. Detroit was considered of minor importance by the British command, and Hamilton, like Clark, failed to obtain the assistance that he requested. His authority did not extend to the regular army troops in the region, and their commander, Sir Guy Carleton, was preoccupied by his efforts to hold the Saint Lawrence valley for the king.[1] Carleton was replaced during the summer of 1778 by General Sir Frederick Haldimand, but the change did little to improve Hamilton's position.

Such British officials in the West as Edward Abbott argued that the use of Indians did more harm than good by driving frontier loyalists into the rebels' camp, and until June 1777 Hamilton was under orders to restrain the Indians from raiding American settlements, while retaining their friendship.[2] Then the British government decided to unleash the red man, and Henry Hamilton carried out his instruction with such zeal that he became known among white settlers as "the Hair Buyer." Hamilton paid well for captives brought to Detroit, and it is doubtful that he actually purchased scalps. But he did give presents to Indians to encourage raids, and indirectly there was some justification for the sobriquet. He was an honest, efficient, ambitious man of considerable cultural and artistic ability, who found himself engaged in tasks that he must at times have found distasteful. But orders were orders, and he executed them to the best of his ability.

When Hamilton learned of the invasion of Illinois he reacted with too great alacrity. The supplies accumulated for the Fort Pitt expedition were available, and he moved swiftly to change the direction of his movement in accord with General Haldimand's order "to employ every means which offers, if not to retrieve the injury done, at least to stop its further progress." By October 7, 1778, Hamilton was ready to leave Detroit with a pickup army that included 33 regular army officers and men, 142 other whites, and 70 Indians. Other Indians were expected to join the force on its way to the Illinois country.[3] It was unfortunate for the British that Hamilton had to depend heavily upon the French militia and volunteers, for with few exceptions he disliked and distrusted them. They were "ignorant Bigots and busy rebels," he complained, and added upon another occasion that he firmly believed there was "not one in twenty whose oath of allegiance would have force enough to bind him to his duty . . . ." He summed up his sentiments by declaring, "To enumerate the Vices of the Inhabitants would be to give a long catalogue, but to assert that they are not in possession of a single virtue, is no more than truth and justice require . . . ."[4]

A fleet of 13 bateaux could carry 39,300 pounds, and 17 canoes and pirogues were capable of taking an additional 33,700 pounds of supplies. Advance parties were sent ahead to construct supply points and to remove obstacles from the route Hamilton had selected. He labored diligently to hold Indian allies and to persuade others to join him on the undertaking. Despite many delays, Hamilton led his men from Detroit on the afternoon of October 7.[5]

They went down the Detroit River to Lake Erie and crossed its southern end to the mouth of the Maumee River. Then they worked their way up the Maumee to Post Miami, the future site of Fort Wayne, where there was a laborious portage to the Wabash River. With unflagging energy, Hamilton overcame all obstacles and drove his men to cover 600 wilderness miles in 71 days. The water level was so low at times that the men had to build dams or use those already constructed by beaver to float their heavily laden boats. Snow fell as early as November 11, and dipping temperatures plagued the troops. "It had frozen hard in the night, and before the men could get at their boats they were obliged to break the ice with poles and then drag in the water up to their knees," Hamilton wrote in his diary on November 22. "In the evening large fires were made and rum was given to the men who had suffered great fatigue and hardship, the ice had greatly damaged some of our boats, a Pirogue in particular was cut thro for the length of 3 feet by which some casks of peas were damaged—."

Indians, both those in the party and tribes along the

way, absorbed much of Hamilton's time and energy, although he was more adept in dealing with them than with the French. He wanted to break camp at two o'clock on the morning of October 8 to take advantage of a calm moonlit night, but his red allies demurred, "saying it was not their custom to travel in the night when they went to War." Hamilton risked his digestion at numerous feasts where the war kettle contained such delicacies as great chunks of fat bear meat, and time after time he sang the war song and performed the war dance in order to gain a few more recruits. Fourteen warriors joined him on November 19 despite a slip on his part. "They said they would follow me wherever I went," he reported, "tho' I had broke thro' an old custom, in not pouring some rum on the Grindstone which was to sharpen the War Axe—I owned myself at fault & ordered two bottles of Rum—This with the delay of issuing provisions delay'd us 'till ten o'clock, when we put off well satisfied with the disposition of our Ottawas."

By the end of November, Hamilton had fairly reliable information about the enemy he was nearing. He knew that a Colonel Clark was at Kaskaskia and that a Captain Helm commanded at Vincennes. Some informants reported as many as 280 of the enemy, and Hamilton received conflicting reports about fortifications at the Falls of the Ohio. Except for the cold, travel was easier after Ouiatenon was reached on the Wabash River, but Hamilton delayed several days in the area to counter American influence among the Indians and to force the French settlers to renew their allegiance to the British crown. When the march began again there was little excitement until December 15, when a four-man reconnaissance party from Vincennes was captured. They were near their goal, and Hamilton sent Major John Hay forward to seize the fort if it was not defended.

When Hamilton arrived at Vincennes on December 17 with the bulk of his command, the American flag was still flying over the fort. But he discovered that most of the

French garrison had abandoned Captain Helm and were turning in their arms to Major Hay's men. The American commander was reported to have only a few loyal men with him.

Deserted by most of his French troops and unable to obtain accurate information until the enemy was upon him, Helm had little choice but to surrender the post. At almost the last minute he scrawled a hasty letter to Clark in which he reported the desertion of the militia and the capture of the spies he had sent out. He had not four men upon whom he could depend. "Think of my condition," he lamented. "Their flag is at a small distance. I am conclude," he scribbled. It was typical of Helm's luck that his letter was intercepted, and it was Hamilton who read it, not Clark. Helm surrendered with dignity, was paroled, and settled down to friendly card games with his captors. Not a shot had been fired in defense of the fort.[6]

Unimpressed by the fort, Hamilton pushed his men hard to put it in a defensible condition as quickly as possible. A well was dug, a barracks completed, a guard-house constructed, the fort itself rebuilt as much as it could be; there was no end to the work that had to be done. On December 19 Hamilton required the French to renew their allegiance by taking a humiliating oath in which they confessed, "We have forgot our duty to God and Man, we implore the pardon of God and hope from the goodness of our lawful Sovereign the King of Great Britain that he will accept our submission. . . ." A white officer kept a party of Indians on the Ohio River, and other scouting parties tried to sever Clark's tenuous line of communications with Kentucky and Virginia. Looking ahead to the 1779 campaign, Hamilton suggested an early spring meeting to John Stuart, the British Indian agent in the South, at which they might coordinate their efforts to squeeze the Kentuckians in a vise.

Somewhat of a puritan in his outlook, Hamilton was annoyed by the "indolent vicious ignorant inhabitants" who changed allegiance as easily as they did clothing. Father Gibault was responsible for much of their bad character, Hamilton declared, but he wrote Haldimand that he was improving the tone of the community by confiscating all of the spirits he could find and by destroying two billiard tables, "the sources of immorality and dissipation" in the settlement.[7]

Much of the British commander's time was devoted to cultivating the Indians in that region, but he was not as successful as he had hoped. The Indians with whom he was dealing had been exposed for some time to the American influence, and it was hard to dispel the respect they had granted the Big Knives. And news of the French-American alliance had had a profound influence among the Indians of the lower Wabash.

In the midst of his myriad activities, Henry Hamilton made the decision that led to his downfall; he decided to winter at Vincennes and to postpone the liberation of the Illinois country until the spring. There were good reasons for his decision. The weather was bad; the land was badly flooded; provisions were in short supply; the Indians needed to be courted; the troops were worn out by their prolonged exertions. Clark was reported to have only a few scattered troops, whose morale was low and discipline lax. Spring would be time enough to complete the conquest; by then Clark might even have fled to the imagined safety of Kentucky. In the meantime, most of the Indians and many of the French were allowed to go home. Hamilton's force that had numbered close to 600 in mid-December had dwindled to some 96 men by the end of January 1779. But he was not concerned. Spring would bring back the manpower he would need.

Clark's intelligence network had failed him during this period. His spies were flung out toward Detroit, but as he ruefully wrote George Mason later, "I kept spies on all the roads to no purpose." When Clark first learned that Hamilton had left Detroit, he assumed that the march was an effort to counter General McIntosh's Detroit campaign—which Clark did not know had long since been abandoned. Correspondence captured along with the British spy at Cahokia hinted that Hamilton was moving toward the Illinois settlements, but the information was so vague that Clark did not act upon it. Although no news came from the reliable Helm at Vincennes, that could easily be explained by the abominable weather. The general atmosphere was disturbing, however, and Clark spent an uneasy Christmas in 1778.

Clark was nearly captured in January by one of Hamilton's detachments. He had decided to concentrate his troops at Kaskaskia if he were attacked, but he wanted to consult with some of the trusted French residents at Cahokia about what their conduct would be if they were subject to British occupation. So in early January, Clark set out for Bowman's fort, accompanied by a small escort and several French civilians who wanted to make the trip. Before they reached Prairie du Rocher, one of the French carts mired down in the muck, and the party was delayed nearly an hour. They were closely watched by some well-concealed scouts from a war party of 30 or 40 men that Hamilton had sent out in an effort to gain information and to capture Clark or others of his command. The scouts decided that the party before them was too strong for them to attack, and when the wagon was finally ready Clark and his party rode on.

They stopped in Prairie du Rocher where Clark was honored by a ball. The gaiety was interrupted near midnight by an express courier who brought the alarming news that Hamilton with a force of 800 men was reported within three miles of Kaskaskia. The fort had presumably come under fire before the courier reached Clark. "I never saw greater confusion among a small assembly," Clark recalled, "every person having their eyes on me, as if my word was to determine their good or bad fate."

Clark made another of his quick decisions. Saddle the horses, he said; he and his men would return to Kaskaskia as quickly as possible. If the fort was surrounded, they would wrap themselves in blankets and mingle with the attackers until there was an opportunity to join the defenders. Clark scribbled a hasty note to Bowman at Cahokia to inform him of the alarm and to tell him to bring reinforcements. Then, to allay the fears of the local citizens, Clark insisted that the dancing resume while the horses were being saddled.

Although there was no sign of the enemy when they galloped into Kaskaskia, Clark assumed that an attack was imminent, and he rushed preparations to repel it. Since he could not defend the town, he decided to burn the portion of it that endangered the fort. If the French volunteers and militia proved reliable, he hoped to be strong enough once Bowman joined him to hold out until Hamilton's Indians became bored with the siege and returned home. But when he consulted with the town's inhabitants, Clark was dismayed by their attitude. While their sympathies were with the Americans, they had concluded that Clark's force was too small for a successful defense. They would be neutral, and they hinted that perhaps he and his men should flee to Spanish protection across the Mississippi.

Clark usually kept his temper under control, "but this declaration of theirs and some other circumstances put me in a most violent rage." He lashed them with "a lecture suitable for a set of traitors" and ordered those in his garrison to leave it. He "must conceive them to be my secret enemies and should treat them as such. . . . I determined to make myself appear to them as desperate as possible, that it might have a greater effect on the enemy." When the Americans started burning the houses close to the fort, the French sought to mollify Clark's rage by stocking the fort with provisions sufficient for a six-month siege.

The situation appeared less desperate by the following day. Captain Bowman arrived with his company and a company of French volunteers. The fort was rapidly attaining a better state of preparedness, and protestations of support came from the French populace. The busy scouts reported that the British "army" had consisted of not more than 30 or 40 men—the party that had nearly ambushed Clark—and they were in full retreat toward Vincennes. It was time for the American commander to display again his skill in handling the French inhabitants. Sensing that they were ashamed of their action, Clark surprised them by not treating them as severely as they anticipated he would. Instead, "I altered my conduct towards them and treated them with the greatest kindness, granting them every request. My influence among them in a few hours was greater than ever; they condemning themselves, and thought that I had treated them as they deserved . . . ."

The period of uncertainty about the status of Vincennes and Hamilton's intentions ended on January 29, when Francis Vigo, a Spanish merchant from Saint Louis, brought the first definite information about what had occurred. Vigo had provided valuable assistance to the Americans from the time of their arrival, and a few days before Christmas he had gone to Vincennes to arrange with Captain Helm for the provisions and ammunition that the garrison needed. Vigo was captured by a patrol as he neared the town, but as a Spanish citizen he was later released. There is a persistent legend that Hamilton first extracted a promise from Vigo that he would do nothing to injure the British cause during his journey home. True to his promise, Vigo was said to have gone first to his Saint Louis home; then he hastened to Kaskaskia to give Clark a full account of the capture of Vincennes, the strength of Hamilton's forces, and the attitude of the civilian population.

Clark and his officers agreed that their situation would be critical by spring, when Hamilton would have such a force "that nothing in this quarter could withstand his arms; that Kentucky must immediately fall, and well if the desolation would end there." They might escape to Kentucky, but they would be overwhelmed there before help could arrive from the East. The only solution they saw "was to attack the enemy in their quarters. If we were fortunate, it would save the whole; if otherwise, it would be nothing more than what would certainly be the consequence if we should not make the attempt." Surprise should work in their favor, for Hamilton would hardly expect an attack in the middle of winter across 180 miles of flooded country. "I was sensible the resolution was as desperate as my situation," Clark wrote Governor Henry, "but I saw no other possibility of securing the country."

The decision made, preparations were advanced with all possible speed. "I would have bound myself seven years a Slave to have had five hundred Troops," Clark wrote afterwards, but he had to make do with what were available. A messenger sped to Cahokia to seek additional volunteers; a company arrived from there on February 4. Packhorses were selected to carry essential supplies, but it was decided that tents would be too burdensome, despite the winter season. A large riverboat was purchased and hastily outfitted as a galley. It mounted two four-pounders and four swivels, and it carried a nine-pounder as well as large supplies of ammunition and food. Captain John Rogers, a cousin of George Rogers Clark, received the dubious honor of being placed in command of the *Willing* and its crew of some 40 to 46 men. He was to take the boat via the Kaskaskia, Mississippi, and Ohio rivers to the Wabash; moving up that stream, he would take station at a point below Vincennes where he could cooperate with the overland party or cut off the escape of Hamilton if he tried to flee southward by water. The *Willing* departed on its circuitous voyage on the afternoon of February 5, 1779.

The overlanders, delayed somewhat by parting ceremonies presided over by Father Gibault, were ready by the following afternoon. They consisted of approximately 170 men, almost the same number that had left the Falls of the Ohio with Clark the preceding year.[8] But upwards of half were now French, the Kaskaskians having asked and received permission to raise a volunteer company to match the one from Cahokia. Some young ladies exerted considerable pressure in helping persuade bachelors to volunteer for service with Clark. Throughout the days of feverish preparation, Clark presented an air of absolute assurance; despite any inward qualms he may have had, he spoke and acted as if success was a certainty. But when he wrote Governor Henry two days before his departure for Vincennes, Clark admitted: "I know the case is desperate, but Sr., we must either quit the country or attack Mr. Hamilton. . . . Great things have been effected by a few men well conducted. Perhaps we may be fortunate."

It was midafternoon when the march finally started, and rain was falling. After crossing the Kaskaskia River, the men marched only three miles before making their first camp. They moved more rapidly thereafter despite swollen rivers and flooded plains, for they were not encumbered with much baggage and the packhorses carried most of that load until the animals had to be abandoned as the column neared the Wabash River. Game was plentiful the first several days and silence was unnecessary; the hunters brought in an abundance of food. Each company in turn hosted the others at the evening meal, and campfire entertainment kept spirits high. The command averaged twenty-five to thirty miles a day for the first six full days of marching, and it reached the Little Wabash rivers on February 13.

Usually separated by three miles, these two streams had been merged into one by the heavy rains and melting snows. Before him Clark saw an expanse of water nearly five miles wide, seldom less than two or three feet deep and frequently more. "I viewed this sheet of water for a time with distrust," Clark admitted, but he soon saw a positive benefit that could be derived from it. Once they were across, they would be so isolated that "all idea of a retreat would be, in some measure, done away." He suspected that the men would be willing to endure almost any difficulty rather than attempt to retrace their steps. With his usual cheerfulness, he treated the crossing as if it were "only a piece of diversion," not a serious problem.

A pirogue was quickly shaped and sent out, like the biblical dove, to find dry land. February 15 was an unseasonably warm day, and the crossing, while difficult, went smoothly. The boat ferried baggage to a scaffolding constructed on the opposite shore, and the horses swam across. The advance party had blazed trees, since the trail was covered with water, and the men slogged their way toward the higher ground found up ahead. The boat carried those who were too ill to walk, in addition to as much of the baggage as possible. A smaller stream was crossed the same way the following day. A small drummer boy helped preserve morale by amusing the troops with his antics as he floated on his drum. Camp was made on some comparatively dry ground, and the men's spirit was good although the supply of food was almost exhausted.

The men were proud of their accomplishment, Clark said; "They really began to think themselves superior to other men, and that neither the rivers nor seasons could stop their progress." They talked of the Wabash River as if it were a creek, and they were confident that they would find a way across it. "They wound themselves up to such a pitch that they soon took Vincennes, divided the spoil, and before bed-time were far advanced on their route to Detroit."

On February 17, so near Vincennes that they could hear the boom of the morning gun at the fort, they encountered flood waters much worse than those through which they had passed. They were near the Embarrass River, and a four-man party was sent ahead to cross it and to seek boats and information on the other shore. The main detachment waded about trying to find the Wabash River, that stream being concealed somewhere in the vast expanse of muddy water that surrounded them. They kept going until eight o'clock in the evening, finally camping on a small piece of muddy ground that was at least out of the water. They made a hungry camp, for their food was gone, and the floodlands appeared destitute of game. An urgent message was sent off to the *Willing;* it should come at top speed. In addition to bringing food, the boat would be invaluable in helping the troops across the nine or ten miles that separated them from Vincennes.

When the four-man scouting party caught up with the main body that night, they reported failure; they had not been able to get across the Embarrass River. The next day Clark led his weary men along the Embarrass until they found its entry into the Wabash. Crude rafts were lashed together for four men who were to seek boats on the far shore. The sodden quartet was never able to find land, and they returned the next morning after spending an uncomfortable night floating on their logs. A canoe was completed on February 19, and Captain Richard McCarthy and three of his men paddled off on a boat-stealing expedition. They returned hastily to report that they had seen four large fires some three miles distant that must belong to the enemy. Clark then sent the canoe downstream to find Rogers and tell him to come on, night and day.

Bowman would never have confessed his fears aloud, but in his diary he wrote: "Starving. Many of the men much cast down, particularly the volunteers. No provisions of any sort now two days. Hard fortune!"

Indomitable as ever, Clark started the construction of more canoes as quickly as possible. Confronted by the desire of the French volunteers to go home, "I laughed at them," Clark said, "without persuading or ordering them to desist from any such attempt, but told them I should be glad [if] they would go out and kill some deer. They went, confused with such conduct." Clark was sure that his Americans would never abandon the enterprise because of hunger as long as horses were available for food, and he knew that if the volunteers could be retained a few days more, the fate of the expedition would have been decided.

The camp was quiet on the twentieth; the atmosphere was dismal, and some volunteers continued to grumble about going home. Then about noon the river guard intercepted a boat from Vincennes and brought in its five French occupants for questioning. Their information, readily given, was heartening. The expedition's presence was not known, and many of the inhabitants of Vincennes were friendly toward the American cause. The captives provided detailed knowledge about the fort and its garrison, and they reported two drifting canoes, one of which was soon recovered. The French hunters came in with a deer that provided some nourishment. It was, Bowman said with his usual understatement, "very acceptable."

At daybreak on February 21 the two available canoes began the laborious toil of ferrying the men across the Wabash River to a hill on the far shore. The horses had to be left behind. It was a slow job, and rain soaked any portions of the men not already sodden from wading. Clark had hoped to reach the town that day after crossing the river, but after leading the way for three miles through water that was sometimes shoulder high, he had to order camp made on another muddy hill. It was again a hungry march. The deer was just a memory, and there was no sign of the *Willing*.

The men pushed on the next day, the weak and ailing being carried ahead to a sugar camp in a maple grove near what had been the banks of the Wabash before it overflowed. Clark was inadvertently responsible for a crisis when he thoughtlessly displayed concern in speaking to an officer of the day's prospects. He was seriously worried about both time and food. "The loss of so much time," he explained later, "to men half-starved was a matter of consequence. I would have given a good deal for a days provisions, or for one of our horses." The men had crowded around, and suddenly "the whole was alarmed without knowing what I said. They ran from one

52

to another bewailing their situation." The long march was near discontinuation at that moment.

But Clark caught the change of mood and reacted quickly. "[I] whispered to those near me to do as I did, immediately took some water in my hand, poured on some powder, blacked my face, gave a warwhoop, and marched into the water, without saying a word. The party gazed and fell in, one after another, without saying a word, like a flock of sheep." Then Clark ordered those near him to start a favorite song, and suddenly the mood was cheerful. A man discovered a path beneath the waters that led them easily to the welcome half-acre of mud that constituted the sugar camp. The captured Frenchmen offered to slip into town and bring back provisions from their homes, but Clark was unwilling to run the risk that their presence might be discovered.

The night was cold, with ice forming on still waters, and some of the troops suffered severely without adequate covering. They were all weakening, and unfortunately the first part of the next march lay across a plain nearly four miles wide that was flooded chest high. Clark plunged into the chilly water after assuring the men that when they reached the woods on the far side of the lake they would be able to see Vincennes. Suspicious of the resolution of some of his followers, Clark placed Bowman and twenty-five trusted men at the rear of the line with orders to shoot anyone who refused to march. The officers expected to lose men that day through sheer weakness, for the effects of hunger and exposure were increasingly visible. But the strongest helped the weakest, and the canoes shuttled back and forth, carrying those who collapsed to the trees ahead. Clark sent a few of the strongest soldiers on in advance with secret orders to shout that the water was getting shallow and that land was in sight, regardless of actual conditions.

It was the most difficult day of their trek. In their condition anyone who slipped beneath the waters was likely to drown, and even Clark found his strength dissipating. But once again the men responded to his exhortations and example and, as he said proudly, "exerted themselves beyond their abilities." Despite his optimistic reports, the water was still chest deep when the woods were reached, but at least the weak could cling to branches or float on logs, while those capable of doing so waded on until they found land. "Many would reach the shore and fall with their bodies half in the water, not being able to support themselves without it." Others found the strength to build fires and to walk their weaker comrades until they had recovered somewhat from their ordeal.

Then, like manna from heaven, some food appeared. A captured canoe carrying Indian women and children also held a half quarter of buffalo, corn, and some tallow. Broth was quickly made and served to those who needed it most. An attempt was made to give everyone at least a sip, but a number of the men insisted that their portions go to those in greater need. This suggestion of food and the fine weather that prevailed wrought miracles in morale. And at last the column halted at a stand of timber called Warriors' Island; from its edge, in full view two miles distant, stood Vincennes and Fort Sackville. Hardships were forgotten in the excitement of that moment.

Clark captured a citizen who was shooting ducks on the plain and learned from him that their presence was still unknown, although Hamilton had been rushing repairs on the fort. Considerable numbers of Indians were reported in the vicinity of the town, and the situation was still critical for Clark's command. He estimated that the enemy could number as many as 600 if the French and Indians supported the British, while he himself was not at full strength and had no artillery because of the continued absence of the *Willing*. If they were defeated, death or capture was almost certain. But they had to have food, and they could not expect to remain undiscovered very long while so near the town and fort. Clark decided on a bold gamble to detach the French citizens from support of the British garrison.

The French prisoner, who had not been allowed to see the size of the command, was sent into town with a letter warning the people that Clark planned to take the fort that night. "I take this step to request of such of you as are true citizens and willing to enjoy the liberty I bring you, to remain still in your houses, and that those, (if any there be) that are friends to the King of England will instantly repair to the fort and join his troops and fight like men and that if such should hereafter be discovered that did not repair to the garrison, they may depend on severe punishment." Anyone found on the streets when his army arrived would be considered hostile and treated accordingly.

News that the Americans were near caused a visible stir in the town as citizens ventured onto the plain to catch a glimpse of the Big Knives. The French assumed that the Americans had come up the river from Kentucky and that the force was much larger than it actually was. But no one informed the British commander of the threat to his position. Toward sundown Clark marched his troops out on the plain, in sight of the town but not of the fort. By circuitous marching around the hillocks that dotted the area and by displaying every available flag and banner, he sought to create the impression of a force that greatly outnumbered the garrison. Since he did not enter the town until after dark, no one there could tell his exact number. And, somewhat to his surprise, there was still no sign of alarm in Fort Sackville.

Hamilton had received some indication of an enemy presence in the area and had made an effort to ascertain its extent, but he could not believe that he was seriously threatened. In midafternoon on February 22 Captain Francis Maisonville had returned from a futile effort to capture some deserters. Taking Colonel Hamilton aside, Maisonville reported that on his way back he had sighted fourteen campfires on the east side of the Wabash, about twelve miles downstream from Vincennes. He assumed that the party consisted of Virginians, but he had not dared go close enough to be sure of their identity or to count them.

"I made no doubt of their being enemies," Hamilton wrote later, and he put the fort's garrison on the alert, ordered the militia under arms, and sent off a scouting party of 20 men to find out more about the mysterious intruders. Soon after the evening roll call was completed, those in the fort heard rifle fire. When Hamilton went onto the parade ground, bullets were passing overhead, but he believed that the firing was being done by drunken townspeople or visiting Indians. The accuracy of the fire soon convinced him otherwise, and Hamilton ordered his men to the blockhouses and the firing platforms along the stockade walls.

The initial firing came from a party of 15 detached for that purpose while the rest of Clark's command occupied the town. The value of local cooperation became apparent immediately when several Frenchmen dug up hidden caches of gunpowder and gave them to Clark. Tobacco's Son, a chief who had openly indicated his friendship for the Big Knives the previous summer, volunteered the services of 100 warriors by morning. Clark did not believe in using Indians, and he feared that his men might not distinguish between friends and enemies among the red men. He thanked the chief, expressed a desire to have the benefit of his company and counsel during the night, but rejected the offer of the warriors.

As Clark reconnoitered the town and fort he discovered that the cannons mounted in the blockhouses had a limited field of fire. His men who got close to the fort were in little danger except from small-arms fire. Breastworks were quickly constructed, and the American riflemen took cover so well that only one or two were even wounded. (These men had the distinction of being Clark's first battle casualties since the command had left the Falls of the Ohio.) But the rifle fire aimed at the gunports was so accurate that several defenders were hit and the cannons were effectively silenced.

Some of the hungry riflemen undoubtedly scrounged food that night, but they were not to enjoy their first regular meal in nearly a week until a welcome breakfast was served the following morning.

With the local French either won over or neutralized, Clark's main concern about possible succor for the fort centered upon the numerous Indians known to be in the general area. To reduce this danger, Clark deliberately allowed Captain William LaMothe's scouting party to slip through his lines and enter the fort near daybreak; they were less dangerous inside the stockade than they would have been outside organizing Indian attacks.

After much of the French militia deserted, Hamilton had some 79 men in his garrison, but he trusted few of them other than his British regulars, and at least six of the latter were soon wounded. Clark had some 170 men, but his only source of reinforcements was the crew of the *Willing,* and that elusive vessel still had not been heard from. The *Willing* also carried all of Clark's artillery, but he thought it imperative that he take the fort without delay. He and Bowman decided that they could undermine Fort Sackville from its river side the following night, unless Hamilton could be persuaded to surrender before then.

Clark sent in a demand for surrender on the morning of February 24, warning his opponent, "If I am obliged to storm, you may depend upon such treatment justly due to a Murderer." If Hamilton destroyed stores, official papers, or houses, "there shall be no mercy shewn you." The British commander refused "to be awed into any action unworthy of British subjects," and the firing that had been suspended was soon resumed. The rifle fire was even more dangerous in daylight, and members of the garrison scarcely dared peer out of cover.

Colonel Hamilton was much perturbed by the attitude

57

of over half his force. When he read Clark's demand to the garrison, "the English to a man declared they would stand to the last for the honour of their Country, and as they expressed it, would stick to me as the shirt to my back. Then they cried God Save King George, and gave three Huzzas." In contrast, "the French hung their heads, . . . [and] some said it was hard they should fight against their own Friends and relations, who they could see had joined the Americans and fired against the Fort———." Their attitude was decisive, and, as Hamilton explained, "I determined from that moment to accept honourable terms if I could procure them."

Toward noon Hamilton proposed a three-day truce, during which neither side would construct works. Clark rejected the proposal, but he agreed to meet Hamilton and Leonard Helm near Saint Xavier, the town's church. Hamilton and Helm were accompanied by Major John Hay, the officer in direct charge of the Indians. The faithful Bowman attended Clark.

At the outset of the conference Clark had an unexpected opportunity to intimidate Hamilton and to convince the watching Indians that their British ally could not protect them. An unsuspecting party of French and Indians that had been raiding toward Kentucky was seen approaching the fort; because of the truce they were unaware that it was under attack. Several of the group were killed or critically wounded and half a dozen were taken prisoner. Two Frenchmen were spared after the intercession of relatives, and a warrior was saved because his father had once befriended one of Clark's officers. The other four warriors were tomahawked and their bodies thrown into the river before Hamilton met with Clark. Hamilton's shock was evident in his written account of the affair. "In consequence I met him on the parade outside the Fort," Hamilton reported; "he had just come from his Indian tryumph all bloody and sweating—seated himself on the edge of one of the batteaus, that had some rainwater in it, & while he washed his

58

hands and face still reeking from the human sacrifice in which he had acted as chief priest, he told me with great exultation how he had been employed."[9] In addition to using the incident to help establish his dominance over Hamilton, Clark saw in the executions a means of convincing the Indians that Hamilton "could not give them that protection that he had made them to believe he could."

During the negotiations that followed, Clark revealed a detailed knowledge of conditions within the fort, including the British commander's inability to rely on the French members of his garrison. The American rejected all proposals for surrender on terms other than his own discretion. Then he warned that his "troops were already impatient and called aloud for permission to tear down and storm the fort; if such a step was taken, many of course would be put down, and the result of an enraged body of woodsmen breaking in must be obvious to him." Clark was again waging psychological warfare, and again it worked.

Hamilton started back toward the fort. Then he turned and asked Clark why he refused to grant terms. Clark replied that he knew "the greatest part of the principal Indian partisans of Detroit were with him; that I wanted an excuse to put them to death, or otherwise treat them as I thought proper; that the cries of the widows and fatherless on the frontiers, that they had occasioned, now required their blood from my hands. . . ." When Hamilton inquired about the identity of such men, Clark promptly named Major Hay as perhaps the worst. According to Clark, Hay was then "pale and trembling, scarcely able to stand"; his fear embarrassed Hamilton, whose own courage had favorably impressed the Americans.

Clark possessed a romantic spot in his soul and Hamilton's dignified conduct somehow touched it. After some moments of silence, Clark said that he and his officers would reconsider the possibility of terms. Meanwhile, the truce would continue. The Americans then decided upon terms that satisfied Hamilton's honor and induced his acceptance. Fort Sackville was to be surrendered intact with all of its stores; the garrison was to march out under arms and with baggage at ten o'clock the following morning, February 25. Officers were allowed to retain necessary baggage, and the vanquished were allowed three days of relative freedom in which to settle their accounts with the local citizens.

Hamilton added a postscript to his acceptance in which he justified his surrender. "Agreed to for the following reasons—The remoteness from succors, the State and Quantity of provisions & c, the Unanimity of Officers and men on its expediency, the Honble terms allowed, & lastly the confidence in a generous enemy." Hamilton was not, at the time of his surrender, in desperate straits, and it seems evident that a more resolute leader might have held out until the arrival of the Americans' artillery.

Guards and patrols remained alert to prevent any incident, but the night of February 24 was the most restful that Clark's men had enjoyed since leaving Kaskaskia so many days and rivers earlier. The surrender ceremony took place as scheduled, and a few minutes later Captain Helm was given the honor of raising the American flag again over the fort. That moment marked the high point in George Rogers Clark's career.[10] Through force of personality and quality of leadership, he had accomplished with surprisingly little bloodshed a feat that most military commanders would have rejected as impossible. But as satisfying as the moment was, his task was still unfinished. Detroit beckoned, and on that February morning it appeared closer to Clark than it had ever been.

4

DETROIT ELUDES CLARK

M UCH REMAINED TO be done after the surrender had been completed. When Clark learned that several British boats were coming down the Wabash with trade goods and provisions, he ordered Captain Helm and a group of volunteers northward to intercept them. Armed with four swivels from the fort, Helm's men ambushed the British flotilla and forced its surrender without a shot fired. The townspeople became wildly excited when the spoils and prisoners reached Vincennes on March 5. The American officers received some clothing, urgently needed to preserve decency, but the remaining cargoes were sold, and the proceeds, amounting to nearly £10,000, were divided among the soldiers. Colonel Hamilton complained bitterly in his journal that Clark did not allow his captives to partake of the wine that had been consigned to them.

The addition of some forty more prisoners complicated what had already become a problem for Clark. Just feeding them would drain limited resources, and guarding them would require too many men. Clark used his instinctive knowledge of psychology to reduce the problem. After frightening some of the French volunteers from Detroit into believing that they were to be taken to the United States, perhaps never to see their families and friends again, Clark suddenly told them he understood that they had been misled and perhaps even forced into joining the British. He was freeing them to return home, if they would promise not to bear arms against the United States until exchanged. He gave them boats and supplies for the long journey home, but some were so overcome with gratitude that they begged permission to join Clark's force. Clark's spies reported that when the others reached Detroit they created such pro-American sentiment that it alarmed the British officers.

Colonel Hamilton and Major Hay were a different matter; their disposition would have to be determined by higher authorities. On March 8 Hamilton and twenty-six other Britishers, escorted by Captain Williams, Lieutenant Rogers, and a score of soldiers, started the long trip that ended in a Virginia prison. Traveling by boat, they reached the Falls of the Ohio on March 30. From there they went overland, with Hamilton complaining of inadequate provisions and transportation. Because of their reputation for buying scalps, Hamilton and Hay may have been in some danger along the way. They spent several days at Harrodsburg, "much against our will thinking we held our lives by a very precarious tenure," Hamilton wrote, "for the people on our first coming looked upon us as little better than savages, which was very excusable considering how we had been represented, and besides that they had suffered very severely from the inroads of those people. One Man in particular had last year lost his son, and had had four score of his horses & mares carryed off, yet this man was reconciled upon hearing a true state of facts, and Colonel Bowman acted as a person above prejudice, by rendering us every service in his power."[1]

Harrodsburg was then momentarily expecting an Indian attack; it would have been strange justice had Hamilton come under fire from warriors he himself might have sent out on the warpath. An astute observer, he noted that as the settlers' number was increasing rapidly, "they will soon set the savages at defiance, being good marksmen and well practiced in the Woods."

Similar treatment was received at Logan's Station, as Hamilton reported. "The people here not exceedingly well disposed to us, & we were accosted by the females especially in pretty coarse terms—but the Captain and his wife, who had a brother carried off by the Indians, were very civil and hospitable." Logan's hospitality could have been a bit forced, for he was then recovering from a broken arm received in an Indian skirmish. A few days after leaving Logan's Station the prisoners and guards passed out of Kentucky, and Henry Hamilton had seen his last of the land to which he had brought so much anguish.

The *Willing* finally arrived at Vincennes on February 27, "the crew much mortified," Clark said, because they had not been present for the fight and surrender. In addition to its welcome load of supplies, the boat carried a messenger who brought Clark the first news and instructions that he had received from Virginia in almost a year. Governor Henry's instructions of December 12, 1778, were already badly dated by subsequent events; but they were couched in general terms, and Clark had been following most of the governor's admonitions. Henry had stressed that "one great Advantage expected from your situation is, to prevent the Indians from warring on this side of the Ohio." Clark was to strive to win the friendship of the Indians, French, and Spaniards. Aware "that your situation is critical" and that communications were difficult, the governor conferred "General Discretionary powers" for Clark "to act for the best in all cases where these Instructions are silent, & the Law has made no provisions."[2]

The messenger also brought a resolution of thanks from the Virginia legislature for "extraordinary resolution and perseverance in so hazardous an enterprise." Clark learned that he would be relieved of much of the burden of civil administration, for the assembly had created the County of Illinois, and John Todd had been appointed head of its government. Clark's success was recognized by his promotion to colonel and Joseph Bowman's promotion to major.

Another piece of information from the East was vital in helping Clark reach a decision not to march at once against Detroit. Governor Henry agreed that "our peace and safety are not secure while the enemy are so near as Detroit," and he was determined to provide Clark with enough men to take that strongpoint. Henry's goal was 500 men, and Clark was told that Lieutenant Colonel John Montgomery should have them in the Illinois country during the spring of 1779. Clark had seriously considered moving on Detroit immediately after the capture of Vincennes, before the British could recover from the shock of Hamilton's defeat. His spies reported that the defenses were in poor condition, the garrison numbered under 100 men, and the French were inclined to favor the Americans. Simon Kenton, who had been a prisoner there, told Clark that Detroit would surrender if he could reach it. "Had I but enough men to take advantage of the present confusion of the Indian nations," Clark wrote Benjamin Harrison, speaker of the Virginia House of Delegates on March 10, "I could silence the whole in two months." He wrote Captain Richard Lernoult at Detroit tauntingly: "I learn by your letter to Governor Hamilton that you were very busy making new works. I am glad to hear it, as it will save the Americans some expense in building."[3]

The prize was tempting, and Clark believed that with 300 men he could take it. But his numbers were limited, and many of his troops were new French volunteers. Some risk would be involved if he moved at once, while his army in the spring or early summer promised to be strong enough to sweep aside all opposition—Montgomery's 500 men, perhaps 300 from Kentucky, additional French volunteers. Prudence won over desire, and the undertaking was postponed. Never again would George Rogers Clark come that close to capturing Detroit.

His decision was to launch the expedition from Vincennes about June 20, 1779. In order to disguise his intentions, Clark decided to move most of his troops back to the Kaskaskia area. He delayed long enough to provide for the garrisoning of the fort and the governing of the town and to conclude treaties with several tribes that had been impressed by his victory. Then on March 20 he left Vincennes with six small boats. The waters were still high, and the travelers moved rapidly until they reached the Mississippi. In a few days Clark was back at Kaskaskia, where the citizens greeted him and his men with joy.

Soon after his arrival Clark learned that some Delawares had killed several traders on their way to Kentucky. He ordered Helm to make an example of the Indians, "to excel them in barbarity." While Helm was to spare women and children, he was to give no mercy to warriors. When the Delaware survivors surrendered, other tribes that had interceded in their behalf were required to be responsible for their future good behavior.

Much of Clark's time and inexhaustible energy was devoted to preparations for the summer expedition. Since little Virginia money was available, Clark directed Captain William Shannon to buy what was necessary by giving "the respective persons furnishing the same notes entitling them to draw on the commanding officer for cash." The supplies were obtained, but Clark endorsed and became responsible for large debts that rightfully belonged to the state. He was never able to collect the sums due him, and his financial embarrassment of later years was largely the result of the obligations he assumed during this period.

Although details are lacking, Clark had apparently done quite well financially except for the debts that he endorsed. He shared the common frontier interest in land, and a war could not blind him to the preservation of his investments. In a March 9, 1779, letter to Patrick Henry he was concerned because the state had set aside land on the Cumberland River for soldiers' grants. "If I should be deprived of a certain tract on that River which I purchased three years ago and have been at a considerable expense to improve, I shall in a manner lose my all. It is known by the name of the 'great french Lick,' on the South or West side, containing three thousand Acres. If you can do anything for me in saving of it, I shall for ever remember it with gratitude."[4] Late that spring in a letter to his father Clark complained about the heavy expenses he had incurred during the campaign in Illinois—at least twelve or thirteen hundred pounds. But he had sent his father ten thousand pounds to hold for him. "If Dicky and myself should both be lost in this Cuntry it will be worth Seven years Trouble of my Brothers to seek after my Fortune which at this time cant be less than Twenty Thousand Pounds Sterling as my success in Trade has been equal to that of War." His father had been aware of his ambitions, Clark continued, "but I did not expect to arrive at that so much determined Moment in so short a time as I have done. Fortune in every Respect as yet hath hovered Round me as if determined to direct me."[5]

By late spring the glowing prospects for a successful expedition began to fade. When Montgomery arrived he had 150 Virginia riflemen instead of the 500 promised, and many of them were in poor condition after having been diverted to an expedition against the Cherokees on the North Carolina frontier. Hoping that something might yet be done, Clark moved his forces to Vincennes in June. He rode easily in four days the miles that had exacted so much effort a few months earlier. He was joined there by Captain Hugh McGary and 30 Kentuckians; he had expected Colonel John Bowman to bring 300. But Bowman had decided to lead his own expedition against the Shawnees at Chillicothe. While he had destroyed part of the town and inflicted several casualties, including Chief Blackfish, Bowman had lost several men and had not crushed the tribe's resistance. Indeed, his raid appeared to stimulate the Indians to even greater efforts.[6]

By midsummer Clark accepted the bitter realization

that Detroit, now much stronger than it had been in February, was beyond his grasp. His dream of taking the British forts on the lower Mississippi also had to be put aside. Supply problems were increasingly serious as Virginia failed to provide adequate funding and the Illinois settlers became more reluctant to sell provisions on credit. Kentucky affairs demanded attention, and Thomas Jefferson, Virginia's new governor, wanted a fort constructed on the Mississippi River. Clark placed garrisons at Vincennes, Kaskaskia, and Cahokia, with Montgomery in command. Then he took the rest of his troops to the Falls of the Ohio. When he arrived there on August 20, 1779, he had been absent from Kentucky for some fourteen months.

Clark soon announced a celebration party that attracted people from several of the interior settlements, although at least some turned back after sighting Indians on the way. But the James Harrods opened the ball in a large room in the new fort that had been built on the south side of the river, and the supply of rum and sugar that Clark had brought back from the French towns kept the party alive for several days. It was perhaps the social event of the year in Kentucky.

Word arrived that the legislature had voted Clark a handsome sword and had set aside 150,000 acres on the north shore of the Ohio near the Falls for the benefit of those who had participated in the campaign. An unhappy piece of news was the death of Joseph Bowman at Vincennes on August 18. Bowman had never recovered fully from an injury received just after Hamilton's surrender. With his death George Rogers Clark lost one of his best friends and most dependable subordinates.

Clark agreed with Jefferson on the need for a fort on the Mississippi, and he spent a good deal of time planning it. Because the area near the mouth of the Ohio was subject to flooding, the site selected was a few miles below that point. Clark estimated that a garrison of 200 would be required, but he thought that at least 100 families would be attracted to its vicinity, and their crops would help supply the troops.[7] When the fort was built in 1780 it was named Fort Jefferson to honor the governor.

As he caught up with the news, Clark found that changes had occurred in Kentucky during his absence. Corn Island had been abandoned at his order, and a sizable community was growing around the new fort. Clark was so impressed by the area's possibilities that he drafted a detailed plan for the future city of Louisville. In the interior of the growing county, Colonel Robert Patterson had begun work on a fort and had laid off the site of Lexington, and Bryan's, Ruddle's, and Martin's stations were started before the end of the year. Land commissioners were expected from Virginia sometime during the autumn; they were to untangle some of the land disputes that plagued the country. While Clark had failed to take Detroit, his presence had thwarted several proposed British expeditions and had set back their plans by a year. The decline in Indian activity that resulted had encouraged migration, and during the fall and spring of 1779–1780 settlers poured into Kentucky. By the spring increasing numbers were daring to erect cabins on their own land instead of huddling behind stockades. Unfortunately, many of them soon discovered that the war was not over.

An October tragedy served notice that the Indians were still dangerous. It terrified many of the newcomers and frightened off some immigrants who had planned to make the river trip to Limestone or the Falls. Colonel David Rogers and 70 men were returning in two keelboats laden with supplies from a lengthy journey to New Orleans. When they reached a point on the Ohio River a few miles above the mouth of the Licking they were surprised by a large band of Indians directed by Simon Girty. Rogers and most of his men were killed. Minor incidents occurred frequently throughout much of the settled area.

Clark remained convinced, as he had told Patrick Henry in April, that "there can be no peace expected from many nations while the English are at Detroit." While he longed to be that town's captor himself, he had also told Henry, "A small army from Pittsburgh conducted with spirit may easily take Detroit and put an end to the Indian war." His qualification, "conducted with spirit," was important. General Washington and Congress drew up plan after plan for such expeditions, but they always failed, usually because of inept leaders. Washington was informed of Clark's progress, and he knew by the summer of 1779 that Clark would not receive enough troops to take Detroit. But Washington had higher priorities in the East, and in October he informed Colonel Daniel Brodhead, then commanding at Fort Pitt, that he could not justify risking an effort against Detroit.[8] That elusive post was left unmolested, and Clark was left to dream of next year, when he might be able to make the attempt at last.

In planning operations, Clark was fond of using formal councils of war. On November 16, 1779, he asked his officers to consider six questions: (1) What troops would be needed to take Detroit or the British posts on the lower Mississippi? (2) How could the troops be provisioned? (3) If they were supplied from Illinois, what would be required? (4) If they were provided by tobacco sent to French and Spanish posts, how much would be required? (5) What forts and garrisons were needed to protect Illinois? (6) What provisions could be expected from Illinois?

After careful consideration, the officers responded that at least 1,000 troops would be needed to take and hold Detroit. A descent of the Mississippi would be easier, especially if Spain declared war on Great Britain, and would require only 500 men. The Illinois country could supply breadstuffs for 500 men, but supplies of meat would have to be procured elsewhere. They could not answer the third and fourth questions, the council said. They recommended forts in the Illinois country in addition to one at or near the mouth of the Ohio. The last would require a garrison of 200 soldiers; 150 would be adequate for each of the others. The forts should be 100 feet square within the walls, which should consist of ten feet of earth eight feet thick, surmounted by a timber stockade also ten feet high. A ditch ten feet deep would surround the fort and supply the earth for the base of the walls. Bastions should be placed at each corner of the structure.

Little could be done during the winter except to draw up such plans. Nature enforced a cold peace upon Kentucky during the "Hard Winter" of 1779–1780. Bitter cold descended upon the country in late November and did not depart until late February. The Kentucky River was frozen two feet deep, and such smaller streams as Salt River were sometimes frozen solid. Maples exploded as their sap froze, and the forests were littered with shattered trees and broken branches. Wild animals perished from the cold and lack of food, and deer and buffalo came into the settlements to contest with domestic animals for the scant supply of forage. Food became so scarce that corn sold for as much as $175 a bushel in inflated Continental currency. A survivor of that harsh winter recalled that "the people were reduced to the utmost extremity for bread, one 'Johnny Cake' (bread baked on a long board before the fire) had often to be divided according to size and number of the family & that only once or twice each day, and even this failed toward the close of winter and for many weeks nothing but meat could be obtained and that poor enough unless a Bear could be found in some hollow tree, which would furnish a feast with Turkey for bread."[9] People huddled by fireplaces as much as possible and longed for spring; a number of them succumbed to illnesses during the endless months of cold.

Spring came at last and brought a resumption of the flood of immigrants that had swelled Kentucky's population during the autumn. In May, Colonel John Floyd wrote a friend about the influx at Louisville. "Near 300 large boats have arrived at the Falls this spring with families. . . . We have six stations on Beargrass with not less than 600 men. You would be surprised to see 10 or 15 waggons at a time going to and from the Falls every day with families and Corn."[10] Before the end of the summer Kentucky's population had grown to an estimated 20,000, a growth that justified its division into three counties—Lincoln, Fayette, and Jefferson. Together they constituted the District of Kentucky, which had its headquarters at Harrodsburg in Lincoln County, the least exposed of the three to Indian attacks. Unfortunately rivalry and jealousy soon arose among the new counties.

Some of the earlier settlers in Kentucky charged that many of the newcomers had a disruptive effect upon affairs in the West. Many of the recent immigrants were held to be inferior to the first settlers. They were said to be poor and discontented, with little interest in anything except good cheap land; they tended to shirk both political and military responsibilities. At least some were Tories who had found it advisable to leave their eastern homes; if they had an opportunity to surrender to the British, they might well do so. A growing number of settlers came from states other than Virginia, and there was increased hostility against Virginia's government. The dissatisfied elements tried to enlist George Rogers Clark as their leader, but he earned their hatred by rejecting their overtures.[11]

When the advent of good weather allowed the war to be resumed in 1780, Clark found himself on the defensive. The British launched a comprehensive plan to retake the western country, and he was concerned with three of the four expeditions designed to accomplish that aim. An expedition of nearly 1,000 men was to sweep southward from Mackinac, capturing both American and Spanish forts along the Mississippi, until it made contact with another force that was to advance up the Mississippi from the Gulf Coast. At about the same time, Captain Henry Bird, one of Great Britain's most effective Indian leaders, was to move from Detroit through the Shawnee country to

Kentucky. Bird expected to take Clark's fort at the Falls, and then subdue the settlements in the interior. A somewhat smaller force commanded by Captain Charles Langlade was to move from Chicago into the Illinois River area. If all went well, the stubborn Americans in Kentucky would be British subjects again before the end of the year.

Confronted by these multiple dangers, Clark reacted decisively. According to one of his biographers, "At no time did he demonstrate in more varied and striking ways his abilities as an organizer and leader of men under adverse conditions."[12] The first blow fell against Montgomery in the Illinois country and de Leyba in Saint Louis. Warned of the impending attack from Mackinac, Clark left Kentucky with a small force and hurried northward. He arrived at Cahokia on May 25, a day before the British, and during a hurried two-hour conference with the Spanish governor, he coordinated their defense efforts. Clark repulsed the British force the next day at Cahokia with little loss; Saint Louis and its environs suffered more severely, although the British also retreated from there and fled northward. Montgomery was sent in pursuit with particular orders to punish the Indian tribes that had participated in the raid. He inflicted heavy damage to crops and villages, but he was unable to pin the Indians down for a decisive defeat before an acute shortage of food forced him to return to his base.

Prisoners taken at Cahokia confirmed the news of Bird's expedition, and Clark left for Kentucky on June 4 in an effort to get to the Falls before the enemy arrived. He hastened back to Fort Jefferson on the Mississippi and ordered every man who could be spared to speed to the Falls by boat. That mode of transportation was too slow for Clark. He and two companions left Fort Jefferson on June 10 on a hazardous trip of nearly 300 miles cross-country to the endangered settlement. According to some accounts, the trio disguised themselves as Indians and were shot at by both Indians and whites on the way.

Bird had learned during the spring that Clark was at Fort Jefferson, and he planned to capture the fort at the Falls before Clark could return, for his arrival would "add considerably to their numbers, and to their confidence." Estimating that Clark might get there between June 14 and July 1, Bird hoped to be ready to attack by June 10. Then the forts in the interior could be overrun. But, he added, prophetically, "if this plan is not followed, it will be owing to the Indians, who may adopt others."[13]

When Bird arrived at the Ohio River, a hundred miles above Louisville, he had nearly 1,000 men in his army, including a good number of whites, most of them French. Such whites as Simon Girty, Alexander McKee, and Matthew Elliott worked closely with the Indians. Their march had been slowed by the two cannons that they carried and the shot and powder needed to service them. When they reached the Ohio the Indians heard rumors that Clark was already at the Falls, and they refused to go there. Unable to change their determination after two days of argument, Bird finally led his warriors against the forts on the Licking River, where many of the settlers were Pennsylvania Dutch. Ruddle's Station surrendered on June 24 after a few cannon shots threatened to demolish the stockade. Bird promised that the settlers' lives would be spared and they would be taken to Detroit as prisoners. The Indians got out of control after the gates were opened, however, and there was some loss of life and a great destruction of property. The wanton killing of cattle led to a serious food shortage within the next few days.

Martin's Station a few miles away soon surrendered on similar terms, and two smaller settlements were either captured or abandoned. The 350 prisoners seriously complicated the supply problem, and Clark was rumored to be on his way to the area. The Indians were surfeited by their easy success, and the punishing raid came to an end. After an extremely difficult journey for the prisoners, Bird arrived in Detroit on August 4 with 150 of the Kentuckians; the remaining 200 were in Indian hands except for those who had perished on the march. At least 13 of Bird's prisoners volunteered for service with the British rangers.

Even as Bird retreated toward Detroit, Clark planned a retaliatory raid to punish the Indians and to deter them from participating in future forays. When he found that Louisville was safe, Clark hastened to Harrodsburg to begin preparations there. He was infuriated by the selfish attitude of many of the inhabitants; they were interested only in land speculation, not in military duty that might protect the outlying settlers. Clark angered many people by closing the land office and posting guards on the Wilderness Road to turn back those who tried to flee to safety with the arms that Kentucky so urgently needed. Clark had no authority to take such action except his own belief that it was necessary.

Although some troops had arrived from Virginia, the success of the expedition depended largely upon the turnout of militia. By working closely with the county lieutenants, Clark was able to assemble nearly 1,000 men at the mouth of the Licking River by the end of July; it was the largest military force ever raised in Kentucky to that time. Supplies were short despite the seizure of a boat-load of provisions destined for Louisville, and there was some grumbling among the men. Not all commanders had had the foresight of Jim Harrod, who had ordered each of his men to bring his own food and had arranged for each mess of six to have a packhorse to carry their supplies.

A John Clary disappeared from Logan's militia, and when his horse was found abandoned at the Licking River, it was assumed that he had fled to warn the enemy. After his forces crossed the Ohio on August 1, therefore, Clark took great precautions to prevent an ambush. He commanded the first division of the army, with Logan leading the second. Supplies and a brass cannon drawn by four horses were placed between the divisions, and far-ranging scouts guarded against surprise attacks. The movement of such a large body could not be concealed, and when the troops reached Chillicothe the Shawnees had fled. Sparing some of the corn for their use on the return trip, the Kentuckians cut down the rest and burned the buildings in the Indian town.

Scouts reported that the Indians were massing at Piqua, some ten or twelve miles distant on the Mad River, so Clark pushed on to that point. Some of the Indians fought in open ranks in European style, and a sturdy log fort held up Clark's advance. But Clark's insistence on bringing the cumbersome cannon paid off, for it drove the Indians out of their fortifications. Logan's division was supposed to cut off the warriors' retreat, but his flanking movement bogged down in rough terrain, and most of the Indians escaped. Clark counted his army's losses at 14 killed and 13 wounded, and he estimated the enemy casualties at triple that number. Clark suffered a personal loss during the battle. His cousin and childhood friend Joseph Rogers had been an Indian captive since his attempt to help deliver Clark's Virginia gunpowder, back in 1776. During the battle he tried to escape from the Indian lines and join the whites, but his shouts went unheeded, and he was shot down.

Crops and homes were also destroyed at Piqua, but the Indians had not been crushed. Clark, still hoping to force a decisive battle, wanted to push on deeper into Indian territory, but because the food supply was almost exhausted and the militia was becoming restive, the command marched for home. When they crossed the Ohio after covering 480 miles in 31 days, an auction was held for the captured goods and the proceeds were divided among the men. Then the army disbanded, and the men returned home to get in their crops, to prepare for fall hunting, and to lie about their exploits.

Clark returned to the Falls to grapple with the problems that had increased during his absence. Robert George implored assistance for Fort Jefferson. He had complained as early as June that he had only 100 bushels of corn left, and he sought permission to issue a shirt to each man to help cover "their naked condition." His situation became even more critical after the fort was attacked by a sizable band of Indians in July. Most of the livestock was killed, and hunting became almost too dangerous to undertake. He tried to feed the destitute civilians as well as his garrison, but when he wrote Clark at the end of July he had only enough corn to last two days. Then he added a postscript that 1,400 pounds of flour and 50 bushels of corn had arrived from the Falls, but he pointed out that it was "a small supply indeed" for 200 people.[14] Farmers in both Kentucky and the Illinois country were increasingly reluctant to sell their produce for depreciated paper currency, and Clark's credit was almost exhausted.

More convinced than ever that the only permanent solution to Kentucky's problem lay in the capture of Detroit, Clark rode east in the autumn of 1780 to seek support for an expedition in 1781. He found a sympathetic listener in Governor Jefferson, who also longed for the reduction of that post and who had full confidence in Clark. Jefferson had already sent Colonel Joseph Crockett to Kentucky with some troops, and the governor had been in frequent communication with General Washington in an effort to secure Continental assistance. Washington would not furnish men and the Congress would not supply money, but the general gave a cautious promise of powder, and Jefferson decided to proceed with plans for the undertaking.

Planning went forward quickly, for Clark had long since worked out his requirements, and on December 13, 1780, Jefferson asked Washington if Virginia could borrow certain military supplies from Fort Pitt for Clark's expedition; they would be returned or replaced. The shopping list ran heavily to artillery and entrenching tools, for Clark anticipated strong fortifications at Detroit. Washington was so eager to see Detroit taken that he did not "hesitate a moment" in ordering Colonel Brodhead to deliver the requested items to Clark if they were available. Brodhead was also instructed to make available some artillerymen and a detachment of such Continental soldiers as he could spare. But he could not recommend Clark for a Continental commission, the commander-in-chief explained, since he was in a state regiment. Washington was not confident of success, since so much depended on unpredictable militia, but he thought Clark well qualified to make the attempt. Even if Detroit was not seized, Washington wrote, "much good will result from creating a diversion and giving the enemy employ in their own country."[15]

Jefferson spent a part of Christmas Day, 1780, penning his final instructions to Clark. To counter the powerful British forces being assembled in the South and West, it was necessary to "throw the enemy under the embarrassments of a defensive war rather than labour under them ourselves." Therefore, as soon as the ice broke on the Wabash, Clark was to undertake an expedition to capture Detroit and control Lake Erie. He would have 2,000 men and ample supplies. An agent had been instructed to purchase 200,000 rations of beef and flour and 100 light barges to transport men and supplies. The soldiers were expected to be at the Falls of the Ohio by March 15. Clark was authorized to build forts if he deemed them necessary, and he was at liberty to move against the Indians if he decided the Detroit plan was not feasible. "Finally," Jefferson wrote, "our distance from the scene of action, the impossibility of foreseeing the many circumstances which may render proper a change of plan or dereliction of object, and above all our full confidence in your bravery, discretion, and abilities, induce us to submit the whole of our instructions to your own Judgment, to be altered or abandoned whenever any event shall turn up which may appear to you to render such alteration or abandonment necessary. . . ."[16]

Soon after receiving these instructions for carrying on the war in the West, George Rogers Clark experienced his only taste of warfare in the eastern theater. Benedict Arnold was raiding on the James River with 1,000 men and inflicting considerable damage. When Clark volunteered his services to the governor, Jefferson sent him to Baron Friedrich von Steuben. Placed in command of 240 men, Clark ambushed a portion of the British force at Hood's Ferry. He killed 17 and wounded 13 before giving way when the British charged with bayonets, a weapon Clark's men did not possess. His service lasted only a few days. Jefferson requested his release on January 13 since urgent messages from the West appeared to require his presence there.

Instead of returning to Kentucky, however, Clark remained in Virginia to supervise preparations for the expedition. He was disturbed by an alleged slight from the Virginia delegation to Congress; they were reported to have objected to his appointment in the Continental Line. Clark was unjust in his suspicions, since Washington had already explained to Jefferson that a law prohibited such a commission for anyone who held a state rank. Jefferson assuaged Clark's concern that he might be thwarted by "some Continental Colonel" by appointing him brigadier general in the Virginia army.

On January 18 Clark wrote Jefferson that nothing more was needed "Except the Mode of paying the Expenses of the Garrison of DuTroit, in Case of Success."[17] Such sanguine expectations soon began to fade in the face of strong opposition to the proposed expedition. The conflict had dragged on at interminable length, and many Virginians were war-weary. Finances were in chaotic condition, and the state itself was almost destitute. By 1781 Virginia was becoming a major theater of the war, and there was a growing demand that all available resources be husbanded for use east of the mountains. When Jefferson attempted to call out the militia to fill Clark's ranks, he discovered that he had almost a mutiny on his hands. The Berkeley County officers, for example, pointed out that they had already sent 70 men to the southern army and had been told to raise 68 more. The 275 designated for Clark constituted half of all that remained, and "we are sorry to inform your Excellency that we have the greatest reason to beleive [sic] that those whose Tour it now is from this County will suffer any punishment, rather than obey our orders for their march."[18] Similar reports forced Jefferson to substitute volunteers for the militia, and Clark's chances of having 2,000 men vanished at that point. The territorial dispute and consequent animosity between Virginia and Pennsylvania reduced sharply the possibility of heavy recruiting from the latter state.

Virginia's decision to abandon her claims to the lands north of the Ohio River also discouraged support for the expedition. Why should the state bear the expense and supply the men to take an area that would soon cease to be Virginia's responsibility? The Continental Congress should assume the burden. As early as February 10 Clark wrote, "I begin to fear the want of men," and the problem became more acute as the departure date neared. Jefferson secured Colonel John Gibson to be Clark's second-in-command, and the governor hoped that Brodhead would allow Gibson's 200 men to accompany Clark. But Brodhead was disgruntled because he had hoped to take Detroit himself, and he took advantage of Washington's order to assist Clark "consistent with the safety of the post" to deny him the use of Gibson's troops.

Discouraging reports came from the West. Nearly 100,000 pounds of beef destined for the expedition had spoiled. Lack of supplies forced the withdrawal of the Kaskaskia garrison, and the soldiers at Vincennes were on half rations. Fort Jefferson had withstood a major attack by the Chickasaws, but conditions there were so bad that Colonel Montgomery abandoned it in early June. He found almost equally bad conditions at Louisville. "The counties of Lincoln and Fayette particularly, tho able to supply us, refuse granting any relief without the cash to purchase on the spot," Montgomery complained. Indian depredations continued. John Todd wrote Jefferson in April that forty-seven people had already been killed or captured that year. "Whole families are destroyed without regard to Age or Sex," he declared. "Infants are torn from their Mothers Arms and their Brains dashed out against Trees, as they are necessarily removing from one fort to another for safety or Convenience. Not a week Passes and some weeks scarcely a day without some of our distressed Inhabitants feeling the fatal effects of the infernal rage and fury of the Execrable Hellhounds."[19]

A shattering blow to Clark's plans came from an unexpected source. In June 1781, Patrick Henry, then a member of the state legislature, secured the passage of a resolution "to put a stop to the Expedition lately ordered against Detroit, and to take all necessary steps for disposing of, or applying to other uses, the stores and provisions laid in for that purpose." Henry had supported Clark staunchly in the past; his opposition in 1781 was aimed more against Jefferson, whose term had just expired, than against Clark. Henry may also have wanted to use all available resources to check the British troops who were harassing the eastern portion of the state. Considerable numbers of Clark's men began to desert at this point.

Hope died hard, but on August 4 Clark admitted that he had "relinquished my expectation relative to the plans heretofore laid." If he could raise troops elsewhere, he would do what he could with them. "I may yet make some stroke among the Indians before the close of the campaign, but at present really to be doubted. I have been at so much pain to enable us to prosecute the first plan, that the disappointment is doubly mortifying to me; and I feel for the dreadful consequences that will ensue throughout the frontier if nothing is done."[20]

If anything could be salvaged, it would have to be accomplished in Kentucky. Several departure dates having already passed, Clark finally left Fort Pitt in early August. He had 400 men with him instead of the army he had anticipated, and he lost numerous deserters on the

trip downstream. Colonel Archibald Lochry was following with some Pennsylvanians, but he did not catch up,
and Clark could not delay too long for fear he would lose
even more men. Aware of Clark's moves, the British had
sent Joseph Brant, the noted Mohawk chief, to intercept
Clark. Brant failed in this attempt, but he captured a small
party Lochry had sent ahead to carry a message to Clark,
and thus learned of the Pennsylvanian's plans and
strength. The Indians surprised Lochry's detachment on
August 24 at a spot a few miles below the mouth of the
Miami River, when Lochry carelessly put ashore on the
north side of the river. Within minutes 107 men were
killed or captured. Some Pennsylvanians voiced the bitter belief that Clark had been responsible for the disaster
or had even planned it.

When Clark arrived at the Falls on August 23, he
realized that he could not even organize an Indian expedition without more help. His commission gave him
authority over Virginia regulars but not over militia unless he had been given express orders by the governor or
was actually conducting a field campaign. Unless the
governor intervened, the militia was subject to the order
of the county lieutenants. There was still magic in Clark's
name and personality, but there was also more opposition
and greater jealousy than in previous years. John Floyd
revealed some of the admiration for Clark when he wrote
Jefferson in the spring of 1781. "The confidence of the
People here have in General Clark's vigilance; his enter-
prising Spirit & other Military Virtues, together with their
inability to remove, have been barely sufficient to keep
this Country from being left entirely desolate." Only the
lack of horses and the fact that the Ohio flowed in but one
direction had kept many citizens from fleeing Kentucky.[21]

The Illinois situation had become critical, with the
French settlers in near revolt. They still admired Clark,
but they liked little else about the American occupation.
In a typical petition to the governor of Virginia the "In-

habitants of Kaskaskia" wrote that they "Humbly profess their loyalty and services to George Rogers Clark, against whom they have no complaint, though the paper money with which he paid them has been found worthless." But they were highly critical of John Montgomery, John Rogers, and the other officers who had been stationed among them. Their property had been seized and paid for, if at all, in worthless currency. When forts had been abandoned, the Americans had carried off the weapons needed to protect the settlers from the Indians who had been incited by the Americans. "If it be thus you treat your friends," one group concluded bitterly, "pray what have you in reserve for your enemies?"

Yet Clark was besieged by desperate pleas for assistance from the commanders of troops still stationed in the Illinois country. Captain John Baley at Vincennes was furious because the inhabitants had surpluses of food while his men were on half rations. He dared not confiscate, since he was badly outnumbered. "Sir," he told his commander, "I must inform you once more that I can not keep garrison any longer, without some speedy relief from you."[22]

Conditions were nearly as bad at the Falls. Two weeks before Clark's arrival Colonel George Slaughter had written the governor, "Unless unexpected and immediate supplies of clothing and provisions are obtained, I shall evacuate this post."[23] Some relief was obtained with Clark's arrival, for he had supplies for a much larger force than the one that came with him. That help, however, was only temporary.

Since whatever action he took would depend upon the militia made available to him, Clark called a meeting of the leading militia officers in early September. Colonels Logan and Trigg represented Lincoln County, Colonel John Todd spoke for Fayette, and Colonels Floyd, Pope, and Cox appeared for Jefferson County. In a formal communication on September 5 Clark reviewed his efforts to take Detroit and the failure of the proposed expedition.

But, he insisted, if nothing was done the Indians would be encouraged to "come on with double Vigour." And nothing could be done unless the militia commanders made a major effort to provide troops. "I wait, as a spectator," Clark said, "to see what a country is determined to do for itself when reduced to a state of desperation. I am ready to lead you on any action that has the most distant prospect of advantage, however daring it may appear to be." Then he added a statement that revealed both his frustration and his determination to lay down the burden he had carried for years. "From some late circumstances, I am apprehensive this will be the last piece of service that I shall have it in my power to do for you in the military line, and could wish it to be as complete as possible."[24]

The colonels could not agree on what could and should be attempted. Clark had suggested an autumn raid against the tribes living along the Wabash, but Logan and Todd argued for a defensive position with a few winter raids launched from a fort that should be built at the mouth of the Kentucky River. Floyd, Trigg, Cox, and Pope favored a fall campaign if it were directed against the Shawnees, whom they considered the greatest threat to Kentucky.

Clark then sought the advice of his Virginia officers. Montgomery, Slaughter, and four captains favored an immediate expedition to the Wabash, but the other eleven rejected that proposal. The group then recommended that the fort at the Falls be held, that another be constructed at the mouth of the Kentucky, and another, if possible, built opposite the mouth of the Miami River. These projects would be possible, they pointed out, only with help from the militia. All the officers, militia and regulars, agreed that aid should be sought from the state for a major expedition against Detroit in 1782.

Logan, Todd, and Floyd promised Clark that they would assist the construction program with men and provisions, but Logan and Todd soon reneged on their word, and Clark received more excuses than help—they had no digging tools; crops were not in; Indians were threatening. A part of their opposition was directed against Clark's firm contention that the Falls was the key to the protection of the whole area for which he was responsible. Not much could be done without the militia, but Clark was unfairly blamed later because he had not completed the forts.

Little in his previous years had prepared the general, rapidly nearing his twenty-ninth year, for the disappointments he endured in 1781. An unusually dejected Clark wrote Governor Nelson on October 1: "I have lost the object that was one of the principal inducements to my fatigues & transactions for several years past—my chain appears to have run out. I find myself enclosed with few troops, in a trifling fort, and shortly expect to bear the insults of those who have for several years past been in continual dread of me."[25] Governor Benjamin Harrison, Nelson's successor, informed Clark that he could request enough militia to bring his total strength up to 304 men—and with them he was to protect the frontier and to garrison forts at the Falls, the Kentucky and Licking rivers, and Limestone Creek.

He would do the best he could, Clark promised, although he was severely handicapped without men, money, and credit. But Virginia's finances were in such condition as to render effective help impossible. Clark was deeply hurt by a resolution of the assembly "to call to account certain officers and others in the western country" for "waste and misapplication of public property." Assuming that the resolution was aimed at him, Clark submitted his resignation. Governor Harrison rejected it, however, declaring that Clark was not the object of the resolution and that he had the governor's highest confidence.

So Clark continued the struggle to make bricks without straw. He would start at once on the Licking fort; he would begin the others as soon as it was possible to do so. Convinced that the Indians would launch massive raids in the spring, he urged the construction of armed river-boats that could be shifted quickly to points of danger. Without governmental funds available, he sold some surplus flour in order to purchase other supplies, then gave his personal bond, secured by a mortgage on 3,500 acres of his land, to replace the flour when more was needed. Small Indian raids caused considerable loss of life and property, particularly in Jefferson County, but there was little that he could do to curb them.

In October 1781, General Cornwallis surrendered a major British army at Yorktown, Virginia, and the war in the East was almost at an end. A treaty of peace seemed certain within the near future. Such developments had little impact in the West. The British would hold western forts for years to come, and they continued to supply the Indians with goods. British officers would cease to accompany and direct Indian raids, but the McKees and Girtys remained available for such direction. George Rogers Clark had been all too correct when he predicted dangerous Indian incursions in 1782. That year became infamous in Kentucky's history as "The Year of Blood."

5

THE WAR ENDS
IN THE WEST

A MILD WINTER IN 1781–1782 allowed some Indian raids to continue during the cold months, and their frequency increased with the coming of spring. News of the defeat at Yorktown did not reach Detroit until April 3, 1782, and then the British commander A. S. De Peyster tried to minimize its significance to the tribes. At a council held in June the Indians decided to eliminate the American settlements before British aid was curtailed. By late summer of 1782 they were striking heavy blows against the Kentucky settlements.

Sure that Indian attacks were imminent, Clark had sought vainly for help that would allow him to blunt the enemy's efforts by attacking first. But in February 1782, Governor Harrison responded to one of the urgent appeals by declaring that the treasury was empty and there was no money for an expedition. "The Executive therefore recommends to the citizens on our frontiers to use every means in their power for preserving a good understanding with the savage tribes, and to strike no blow unless compelled by necessity." Such advice was cold comfort for the Kentuckians who were enduring increasingly severe raids before the governor's letter arrived.

Despite the obvious danger to their people, many Kentucky leaders could not be persuaded to cooperate effectively to repel the enemy. By 1782 Kentucky's population and resources might have been adequate for the task without extensive aid from the Virginia government if the efforts had been fully supported and carefully coordinated. But such cooperation was not forthcoming. The populace had become increasingly heterogenous, and petty quarrels and personality conflicts prevented the close cooperation that the situation demanded. Clark did not have the authority to force the militia to assist him, but he was readily available as a scapegoat when things went wrong.

Prevented from carrying the war to the enemy, Clark endeavored to construct the forts and boats that might place a defensive shield above the Kentucky settlements. When the governor reported that "we have but 4 shillings in the treasury and no means of getting any more," Clark and Floyd somehow succeeded in getting a boat built at the Falls. With a keel of 73 feet, it carried 46 oars, several cannons, and a crew of over 100. The sides were musket-proof, and hinged gunwales could be raised so high that the boat could venture close to shore without the danger of being fired into. The craft was available in early July, but Clark had difficulty in manning it. Some of the militiamen assigned to it refused to go on board, "alleging that Militia could not be made Salors of," and volunteers had to be recruited for the purpose. Clark stationed the vessel near the mouth of the Licking River where its presence deterred Indians from crossing to the Kentucky shore for fear they would be trapped there.

Although unable to launch an expedition against them, Clark did what he could to convince the Indians that he was about to attack them at some point. Alexander McKee boasted that he and others had assembled in the Shawnee country the greatest number of warriors brought together since the start of the war, but rumors that the chief of the Big Knives was preparing to take a large force to Detroit delayed their move. Imaginative Indian scouts reported that Clark had a large army at the Falls, and other scouts magnified the group of militiamen who had refused to become sailors into the advance guard of a large army that was moving up the Ohio. Suspecting that they were the object of that army's movement, most of the Shawnees refused to cross the river.

When William Caldwell and McKee crossed into Kentucky they had some 50 rangers and 300 Indians instead of the force triple that number that they had expected to lead. But the militia commanders in Kentucky had been negligent in providing for scouting, and the enemy was able to penetrate nearly one hundred miles into Kentucky without being discovered. They appeared at Bryan's Station, a few miles from Lexington, on August 15, three days after they had defeated a party of 18 whites at Upper Blue Licks. The station's 44 fighting men beat off all attacks until the Indians retired two days later after burning outlying buildings. The enemy moved leisurely to the northeast, apparently in anticipation of pursuit. At Blue Licks, thirty-odd miles northeast of Lexington, they prepared an ambush after crossing the Licking River.

Messengers had carried word of the attack on Bryan's Station to other settlements, and help was hurriedly assembled there. Colonel Trigg brought 130 men from Lincoln, and Colonel John Todd collected some Fayette riflemen. Logan was coming with additional troops, but Todd moved out in pursuit of the Indians on August 18 with 182 mounted men. Although Boone and some others may have warned of danger, an impetuous charge was made across the Licking River without adequate reconnaissance or proper planning; many of the men and officers apparently feared charges of cowardice if they insisted upon a cautious approach. The Indians sprang their trap, and within minutes Kentucky had experienced her worst defeat of the war. Over a third of the Kentuckians were killed, among them Todd and Trigg, and a number of badly wounded men had to be left behind. The Indian casualties numbered less than a score. When

Logan met the fleeing survivors, he retreated to Bryan's Station. Only when he had accumulated 470 men did he advance cautiously to the site of the massacre. The enemy had long since disappeared, and Logan could do nothing but bury the dead.

Clark had been many miles from the debacle, and he acknowledged no blame for the tragedy. The Indians' success was due, in his opinion, to the lack of adequate scouting that would have revealed their presence in the area and to "extremely reprehensible leadership." The latter he blamed on foolhardy efforts "to offset . . . former neglect of duty."[1] But in an effort to shift the burden of guilt, several militia commanders blamed Clark for the defeat. When Logan wrote his account for the governor he distorted and omitted facts to put Clark in a bad light. While he had supplied men to build a fort at the Licking River, Logan complained, they had been sent to Louisville and used there. He did not report that he and Todd had rejected Clark's original call for men to construct a fort at the mouth of the Kentucky. Nor did Logan admit that the boat had been sent upstream from the Falls and that he had voted for the defensive posture that he now criticized.[2] Boone was even more direct in his attack. After asking that 500 men be rushed to Kentucky, he requested that they be placed under the command of the county lieutenants, for "if you put them under the Direction of Genl. Clarke, they will be Little or no Service to our Settlement, as he lies 100 miles west of us, and the Indians north East, and our men are often called to the Falls to guard them."[3]

Such charges and insinuations ignored the fact that Jefferson County was also enduring attacks. Kincheloe's Station was surprised on September 2 by a band of 100 warriors who captured 37 settlers. The parochial attitudes that the criticism implied reflected a vital difference between Clark and some courageous, skilled woodsmen of limited vision. More than any leader in the West at this time, Clark saw the overall dangers and opportunities. He had both concern and responsibility for the Illinois country as well as for Kentucky, and with his base at Louisville he was in a much better position to deal with both than if he had acceded to demands that he move eastward. Much of Clark's frustration came from his inability to get others—whose help he had to have—to see the possibilities that were so plain to him.

Clark had a number of determined personal enemies in the Virginia legislature, and some of them seized upon the charges in an effort to discredit him. In addition to complaining about his military incompetence, they circulated rumors that Clark was a drunkard. "General Clarke is in that country," Colonel Arthur Campbell wrote one of the governor's secretaries, "but he has lost the confidence of the people and it is said become a sot; perhaps something worse."[4]

Governor Harrison, perhaps fearing that he might be blamed for the defeat because of his neglect of the West, hastened to accept such reports. Ignoring Clark's frequent requests for men, money, and materials, Harrison accused the general of failing to carry out orders to build the forts on the Ohio. In a typical charge he wrote Colonel William Fleming, the chief commissioner of western military accounts: "I gave the General orders in December last to build forts at the mouth of the Kentucky, Licking, and Limestone and to garrison each of them with sixty eight men. If he had obeyed the orders, it is probable that the late misfortune would not have happened." The governor had also adopted the drunkenness charges. "A report, much to his prejudice, prevails here of his being so addicted to liquor as to be incapable of attending of his Duty, by which the public interest suffers much." Fleming was asked "to inquire into this in a private way, and let me know your sentiments."[5]

Clark did not hear for some time of the vilifications being circulated against him, and he was sure that the strengthening of Fort Nelson and the Kentuckians' knowledge of the Indians' plans had saved the western country. Had it not been for "that imprudent affair" at the Blue Licks, the enemy would have caused little trouble.[6] That event had at last aroused the people from their selfish apathy, and Clark was begged to lead an expedition against the Indians responsible for the defeat. Although offensive action had been prohibited by the Assembly, Clark assumed that the government would accept the need for swift punitive action. The county lieutenants cooperated by calling out the militia, and assembly points were set at Bryan's Station and Louisville.

When the whole force reached the mouth of the Licking on November 1, Clark commanded 1,050 riflemen. Since most of them were militia, he took particular pains to prepare detailed written orders and to make sure that every man knew just what was intended. Plans were made for almost every contingency. If the column should be attacked, for example, the section hit would try to hold its ground and the attention of the enemy while the other elements immediately began a flanking movement. The cannon that had proved so effective two years earlier was again carried with the troops.

Despite the impediment of the cannon and the need for caution, the expedition had reached the heart of the Indian territory along the Miami River by November 10. But the Indians would not engage in a decisive battle, and the fighting consisted of minor skirmishing. When Clark totaled the casualties, he had lost one man killed and one wounded; "The loss of the enemy was ten scalps, seven prisoners, and two whites retaken. . . ." Old Chillicothe had not been rebuilt after its destruction in 1780, but the Kentuckians occupied New Chillicothe (Piqua), McKee's Town and a number of other points. Small raiding parties spread out over the countryside to inflict maximum damage when it became apparent that they faced little opposition. Boone took a hundred men to Willstown, where a large cache of furs was found. Those that could not be carried off were burned. Logan led a somewhat larger force that captured Loramie's Trading Post, an important supply point for the Indians. Pierre Loramie escaped, but the post was burned, and a wealth of trade goods was brought back to the main body.

After four days spent wreaking destruction over a broad area, Clark ordered a withdrawal to the Ohio. Little more damage could be done in that ravaged area, and the Indians were determined not to risk an engagement. Cold, wet weather was threatening, and the troops were not equipped for a winter campaign. The plunder was auctioned and the proceeds divided. The expedition reached the Ohio on November 17, and the army was disbanded.

Clark had hoped to coordinate his expedition with one led by General William Irvine against Sandusky; perhaps their joint effort could capture Detroit. But Irvine's march was canceled by General Washington after he was assured by British authorities that they had ceased to sponsor Indian raids. While he had not smashed the Indian strength, Clark's raid slowed Indian attacks for several months. As Daniel Boone testified before a committee of investigation in 1787, "The spirits of the Indians was damped, their connexions dissolved, their armies scattered, and a future invasion (was) entirely out of their power."[7] But the curtailment of British support probably had as much to do with the slowing of Indian forays as did Clark's 1782 expedition.

Governor Harrison's letter of congratulations belied his recent disapproval of Clark, but in view of the paucity of support from the East, the general may have discounted other sentiments expressed in the governor's message. "It has ever been my Opinion," wrote the governor, "the attacking of them in their own Country is the only way to keep them quiet, and save expence, but I have unfortunately differed in Sentiment from those to whom I am amenable. . . . I have now, Sir, to return you my particular thanks and those of my Council for your spirited and judicious Conduct through the whole course of your

Expedition, and to assure you that we shall ever entertain the highest Sense of the Important Services you have rendered your Country. . . ."[8]

Once back in Kentucky, Clark learned of some of the complaints about his measures and conduct that had been sent to the governor, but believing that he possessed Harrison's confidence, he resumed his efforts to protect the Kentucky settlements. He was anxious to do as much as he could as soon as possible, for before the expedition he had asked "to be relieved from this department." Soon after his return, Clark suggested to Harrison that a spring raid against the Wabash tribes might end the troubles from that quarter. "If you should think of putting any such thing in execution," he volunteered, "I shall yet receive pleasure in making every preparatory stroke in my power, before I leave the country, which I hope will be the last of March."

Then on the last day of November 1782, Clark received a letter that revealed how seriously his status with the governor had been undermined. Harrison censured him sharply because no messages had been received for several months. "Government can never be administered properly unless the officers of it are regular in their description of the wants and distresses of their departments," the governor complained. He had heard of the disaster at Blue Licks, and "these are circumstances so much within your line of Duty, that I cannot help expressing my very great surprise at your Silence." Clark had been ordered to erect three forts and to garrison each with sixty-eight men. Harrison did not know what had been done, "but I have every reason to suppose from other information that they have altogether been neglected, to which much of the present misfortune is to be attributed. . . . it gives me great pain to find that you have disappointed us in our expectations. . . . I insist that they be carried into immediate execution. . . ." In case of "urgent necessity" Clark could draw up to 200 men from Washington, Montgomery, and Botetourt counties. He would do well, the governor warned, to consult with the commissioners of western accounts about his problems. He should also submit all of his military accounts to them. When that was done, Harrison added, "I shall expect your attendance here for a final settlement of them."[9]

Clark must have been infuriated when he read the unjust accusations, but he exercised remarkable restraint in answering Harrison's letter the day it was received. He had informed the government of all but the most trifling events, but the Indians had interfered with messages in recent months. In a previous letter he had explained fully why the forts had not been constructed. In his efforts to build them, Clark charged, "I had not only to counteract the designs of the enemy, but a powerful party endeavoring to subvert the Government, of which, I have reason to believe, a great part of those who give your Excellency so much intelligence belong." He had never had enough men to build and garrison the forts. As to the Blue Licks defeat, Colonel Todd's militia had been given only scouting duties to warn of the enemy's approach. "Instead of those necessary duties being done, on which their salvation apparently depended, the enemy was suffered to penetrate deliberately into the bowels of their country, and make the attack before they were discovered. This, I believe, is what is wished to be blinded, and the neglect to be one of the principal springs to that mad pursuit and carnage of the Blue Lick, as the reverse of fortune could have obliviated their former neglect." He had not reported details, Clark said, that would have hurt the reputations of those who participated in the disaster.

The governor was being misled, Clark warned, and "as long as you countenance those kind of people, you encourage enemies in the state and keep your government in confusion; but I know your situation and how difficult it must be for you to discriminate." Clark thought that he had "perhaps experienced greater anxiety for the welfare of the State than most of the men in it...." He was obviously hurt by the tone and contents of Harrison's curt letter.

In a letter written a few days before Christmas, Governor Harrison repeated his strictures about building the forts, but he concluded with the permission to resign that Clark had sought: "I agree with you that the Command you have is not a proper one for a Gentleman of your rank, and therefore accept your proposal of resigning it." Before coming east, however, Clark should reduce the forces to a number commensurate with peace.[10] With the coming of peace in the East, Virginia's military establishment was to be reduced without regard for the continued needs on the Kentucky frontier.

While Clark was pleased by the permission to retire, he corrected the governor on the reason he had cited; he did not seek retirement, Clark asserted, because of the size of his command. He saw a group of people trying "to divide the counsels of the people here, and at the same time destroying their interest at the seat of Government," and they were succeeding in their efforts. He was one of their targets, and he did not want "to be a witness to the great success of their attempts against me. . . . I wished to be clear." As further proof of his inability to build the forts, Clark reminded the governor that because of lands he owned along the Kentucky River he would have profited personally had he been able to erect a fort at the mouth of that stream.[11]

The tone of Harrison's letters began to change. He was "fully impressed with the services you have rendered your country on many occasions," he assured his commander in the West. The smallness of his command was the only reason he had acceded to Clark's request to resign. His enemies had never injured his reputation materially with the Executive. Clark was still not aware of the damaging questions and insinuations contained in Harrison's letters to others.

Until the day of retirement came, Clark's sense of duty

and responsibility kept him concerned with the still-essential problem of defending Kentucky. The population was growing, new counties were being created, agitation for statehood was increasing, towns were being established—and citizens were still being killed by Indians who slipped across the Ohio into the Dark and Bloody Ground. Despite the end of the war with Great Britain and the progress made toward concluding a treaty of peace, military conditions in both Kentucky and Illinois continued to deteriorate. If the war was over, why was it necessary to supply men and money for a military establishment on the western waters? The economy of eastern Virginia was in a desperate state, and only a determined effort could have raised the support Kentucky needed; such an effort was not made. The continued threat to Kentuckians was emphasized to Clark in early 1783 when his loyal friend and supporter John Floyd was killed by Indians in Jefferson County. In 1790 it was reported that 1,500 Kentuckians had been killed and 20,000 horses stolen between 1783 and 1790.

In early January of 1783, Clark wrote that there was not "a Ration to be got on the Credit of the State," and the supplies accumulated for the ill-fated 1781 expedition had been exhausted. "If the soldiers could receive but a part of their pay, it would encourage them greatly," he added in an understatement. In February the remaining officers of the shrunken Illinois Regiment reported to their commander on the "present deplorable situation of the garrison." It had only a third of the number needed, and that number would soon drop, perhaps as low as 20. The supply of flour would not last three months, and there was no meat and no prospect of getting any. Their lead would not last a day in case of a serious attack, and parts of the fortifications were falling into disrepair. The men were on the point of mutiny after going so long without pay and other necessities. Unless something was done soon, the officers warned, Fort Nelson might have to be abandoned.[12]

Clark tried to impress the Board of Commissioners with the seriousness of the problem his officers had described: "The Troops formerly a Barrier, reduced to a handfull, the credit of the State sunk; not a shilling of money, not a Ration to be procured any other way than by voluntary advances from a few individuals." The Illinois country might soon be lost, and that would double the number of Indians left free to attack Kentucky. The Kentuckians were "too few in number to harrass [sic] the Enemy, in the manner it ought to be done, and too great a number of women and children to make their escape from the Country." A fall invasion was certain, Clark warned, unless something was done soon to prevent it. With some assistance, Fort Nelson could be held and one or two other forts built along the Ohio. But Clark placed his chief reliance upon a July expedition that would crush the tribes' ability to wage war. Kentucky might furnish as many as 1,000 men, he estimated, but another 500 would be required. Given 1,500 men, the job could be accomplished in two months at little cost. Clark had small faith in British promises to restrain the Indians; they had to be taught to fear the Americans.

Clark's skepticism remained even after he heard in April 1783 of the peace treaty that had been drafted. "The prospects of our possession of the posts of the lakes will, I make no doubt, divide the Councils of the Indians for some time," he admitted, "and prevent their making any capitol stroke on the Settlement of Kentucky." But he doubted that some of them would make peace unless given presents or forced to do so by an invasion of their country.[13] And Clark, as always, was opposed to efforts to buy Indian friendship.

The terms of the British treaty delighted Clark, however, particularly those that set the boundaries for the United States. Detroit that had eluded him for so long was now a part of the nation. Both some of his contemporaries and some later historians concluded that the United States had gained the Northwest because of Clark's exploits there in 1778–1779. Although Benjamin Franklin, and presumably the other members of the American delegation, had known of Clark's conquests since 1779, there is no evidence that any reference was made to his success during the course of the negotiations. Franklin argued that the frontiersmen would be troublesome neighbors if the British retained that region, and he urged acceptance of a generous boundary that would encourage better relations between the two countries. Lord Shelburne accepted this proposal, but he would hardly have done so had the British been in firm possession of the lands north of the Ohio. It is wrong to give Clark too much direct credit for the nation's acquisition of the Northwest; it is equally erroneous to deny him any influence on the disposition of that territory. While Clark had been forced to pull back his troops from much of the area, he was always conscious of its importance, and from his Louisville base he could move quickly to thwart a British invasion.[14]

Sometime during the late spring Clark rode through the wilderness to Richmond to settle his accounts and relinquish his commission. The commissioners of western military accounts had already approved two claims: his officer's pay, dating back to January 2, 1778, and the flour he had personally acquired for the Fort Nelson garrison. The total value was £3,397.16.5½. Many of his vouchers had disappeared into the bureaucratic maw at Richmond; some 2,000 of them would not be found until 1913. Clark was so destitute in 1783 that when he reached Richmond he asked the governor to advance him a small amount against his account. "I am exceedingly distressed for the want of necessary clothing, etc." Clark explained, "and don't know of any channel through which I could procure any except that of the Executive. The State, I believe, will fall considerable in my debt."[15] Since Virginia had little or no money, Clark was paid in military certificates and warrants.

While Clark was trying to clear his accounts, he continued to urge Harrison to order an expedition against the tribes north of the Ohio. Clark also presided over a late May meeting of Virginia officers who were seeking settlement of their claims against the state, and he was chosen to supervise the selection and disposal of lands that might be assigned to them. He spent a good deal of time with his family, and his love for Kentucky so infected his parents that in 1784 they moved to Mulberry Hill, an estate near Louisville. Clark was concerned about his own financial condition, but he may have been even more upset by the financial plight of such men as Oliver Pollock, men who had ruined themselves trying to help him. It added to his growing sense of frustration that he was unable to help them.

Clark welcomed a letter from the governor, dated July 2, 1783, that the Executive Council had authorized the previous day. An Indian expedition was economically impossible, the governor wrote, "which you will easily perceive will render the services of a general officer in that quarter unnecessary, and will therefore consider yourself out of command." But, Harrison continued graciously, "I feel myself called upon, in the most forcible manner, to return you my thanks and those of my Council, for the very great and singular services you have rendered your country in wresting so great and valuable a territory out of the hands of the British enemy, repelling the attacks of their savage allies, and carrying on a successful war in the heart of their country."

For the thirty-year-old general, the war had at last come to an end.

6

THE AFTER YEARS

GEORGE ROGERS CLARK lived too long for the good of his reputation. The apex of his career was reached at Vincennes on February 25, 1779, when he accepted the surrender of Henry Hamilton. Although he performed valuable services between that time and the date of his separation from military service in 1783, his detractors succeeded in tarnishing his reputation before he resumed civilian life, and his postwar years diminished rather than enhanced his renown. Only occasionally after 1783 were there glimpses of the man who had displayed exceptional qualities of leadership during the war. His traducers must have enjoyed witnessing his decline. Men scorned and insulted him who had fawned for his attention a few years earlier.

His precarious financial and legal condition rendered a business career impossible. Many years after his death, Clark's estate received some $30,000 from Virginia in at least partial discharge of the state's debt to him, but during his lifetime Clark was hounded by creditors for debts he had contracted on behalf of the state. Since his property was subject to seizure, the family agreed to take care of him, and what holdings he had were concealed as much as possible in family property and enterprises.

Clark dabbled in a number of undertakings, but none was worthy of his talents, which rusted in disuse. The

Virginia officers elected him superintendent-surveyor to select, survey, and allocate the lands granted to them, and Clark retained that position until 1788, although he did not devote much personal attention to it.

Some of his best work was done in Indian negotiations, a field in which he had few peers. His reputation remained higher among the Indians than in Kentucky and Virginia, and he continued to exert a great deal of influence with the tribes. Despite the provisions of the peace treaty, the British continued to occupy Detroit and a number of other posts, from which the United States government was not strong enough to dislodge them. Indians continued to inflict damage in the Kentucky counties, and the impending migration of settlers in large numbers across the Ohio would lead inevitably to conflict unless the Indians could be persuaded to relinquish at least part of their lands to the axe and plow of the frontiersman.

Clark was one of the United States commissioners who met with representatives of several tribes at Fort McIntosh in early 1785. The Indians present agreed to give up Shawnee lands in southern Ohio, but Clark was not able to persuade the Shawnees themselves to participate in the councils until January 1786. Negotiating with his vast knowledge of the Indian mind and using other tribes skillfully to exert pressure on the reluctant Shawnees, Clark was largely responsible for the treaty that was signed on February 1. But the Indians soon formed the Wabash Confederacy to drive out the whites, including even the French, who had usually been immune to Indian attacks. Vincennes was threatened for three days, and several lives were lost in Kentucky as small raiding parties again crossed the Ohio into Jefferson County. Clark was one of fifty-five prominent citizens who sent an urgent plea for help to Colonel Logan, who forwarded it to Patrick Henry. "I don't think that this country, even in its infant state, bore so gloomy an aspect as it does at present," Clark warned Governor Henry, predicting that a "great part of these beautiful settlements will be laid waste unless protected by volunteers penetrating into the heart of the enemy's country. Nothing else will do."[1]

As the raids spread into other Kentucky counties, demands increased for Clark to come out of retirement and lead another expedition. The matter was complicated by Virginia's cession of the lands beyond the Ohio; was that area not now the responsibility of the United States government? Did Virginia have the right to send her militia outside her boundaries unless requested to do so? But Congress balked at the expense of an expedition, and the militia officers in the western counties of Virginia were told to take action if necessary to defend themselves. Henry warned Congress that an expedition against the Wabash Indians was likely; he was not told to prevent it. Patrick Henry's close friend and brother-in-law, William Christian, had been killed in Jefferson County by Indians, and Henry may have felt a closer personal involvement than he had in the past.

Clark refused to step forward until he was assured of support in Kentucky, but by midsummer he was preparing to march. "I expect to leave the Falls on the First Day of August with fifteen hundred men," he wrote an agent of Congress, "determined not to return without destroying their country, or reducing them to terms on our own. . . ."[2] Clark was concerned about having to depend largely upon drafted militia instead of volunteers, but he accepted the request of the militia officers that he lead the army. Their draft was designed to procure 2,500 men with provisions for 50 days and a packhorse for each 4 men. The soldiers were to assemble at Clarksville on September 10.

Doubts continued about the legality of the expedition, and opposition to the draft was strong. By September 12 only 1,200 men were present at the rendezvous. Some officers were sent back to their counties to round up the missing troops, but the rest decided to move without waiting for reinforcements. Clark preferred to march directly against the Wabash tribes, some 150 miles northwest of Clarksville; others insisted that they go first to Vincennes, where they could receive supplies and information. When Clark refused to command if his orders were limited to Vincennes, that provision was removed, but he agreed to go there first. Aware that the Shawnees were again on the warpath, Clark sent Benjamin Logan against them with the additional troops being raised in Kentucky. Many of the Shawnee warriors had gone westward to help stop Clark, and Logan's raid destroyed a large amount of property with minimal loss.

Some of Clark's men and supplies were forwarded to Vincennes by boat; the rest of his force marched there. Grumbling was constant from the outset, especially among the Lincoln County soldiers. Against his better judgment, Clark was forced to remain in Vincennes until the boats arrived. The days thus wasted delayed his campaign, allowed morale to deteriorate further, and consumed more supplies than the boats carried.

When the army finally moved, discipline was poor and insubordination evident. As they neared the Indian towns the Lincoln County militia refused to proceed, complaining that food supplies were inadequate. Clark made a personal plea for their support. "Only promise me," he begged, "to go with me two days march, & if I don't furnish you with as much provision as you want, I will return with you." The mutineers were oblivious to his pleas, and they left him there, tears streaming down his cheeks.[3]

The other commands voted to follow wherever he led, but Clark and his officers decided that their remaining force was too small to risk in an attack, and they retired to Vincennes. The Illinois country was in danger of being overrun but Clark bluffed the Indians and concealed his weakness. He had withheld his destruction when he was near their towns, he told the tribes, because he wanted to give them one last chance to prove their good intentions.

103

If they rejected his offer of peace, they could expect white families to move in to occupy their lands. The Indians were slow to respond, and supplies were dangerously low, although by a court-martial Clark confiscated a cargo belonging to some Spanish merchants, a move that later led to charges of illegal action.

The Indians feared to attack Vincennes with Clark there, and they could not raid into Kentucky with him on their flank; at the same time Logan had at least temporarily immobilized the Shawnees. The Indians finally asked for a council, and peace was arranged in the spring of 1787. It was Clark's last important negotiation with the Indians, who had learned both to fear and to respect the chief of the Big Knives.

When Clark arrived home he found that malcontents were blaming him for the failure of the expedition. A particular charge, one that had been used earlier, was that his drunkenness had incapacitated him for effective command. There is no doubt that Clark drank in an era when drinking was commonplace, and there is no doubt but that he became increasingly addicted after the late 1780s. But there is little evidence beyond gossip and rumors that the failure of his last expedition was due to intoxication. Such men as James Wilkinson, who was attempting to undermine Clark's position by destroying his reputation, were apparently responsible for spreading the malicious accusations.

When Clark learned of the charges being circulated against him, he demanded an official inquiry, but Governor Randolph ignored his request. The Virginia Council, without seeking his defense of his actions, condemned Clark both for the expedition and for many of the actions he had taken in connection with it. Public proclamations disavowed his efforts and invited individuals to take action against him. After this outrage, Clark sought oblivion from his disappointments in alcohol. But men who knew him well had had no doubt of his capabilities as late as 1786. John May of Vincennes wrote Patrick Henry on

July 14, "I have been with him frequently, and find him as capable of business as ever, and should an expedition be carried against the Indians I think his name alone would be worth half a regiment. . . ."

Wilkinson, anxious to remove Clark as a possible obstacle to his schemes, persuaded ten prominent Kentuckians to send a letter to Governor Randolph. In this letter, dated December 22, 1786, they called Clark "utterly unqualified for business of any kind" because of his alleged addiction to liquor.[4] That calumniation soon became true. George Rogers Clark had struggled with adversity for years; suddenly his resiliency was gone. Physically, mentally, psychologically, he was no longer the man he had been. Bitter over his neglect, disappointed over the lack of support, frustrated in his effort to achieve total victory, Clark found solace in the whiskey that Kentucky was producing in increased quantity.

Clark's health was poor, and his finances continued in a precarious condition with creditors pressing for payments that should have come from the state. In his anger and frustration, Clark turned to several projects that led many people to question his loyalty. One abortive scheme involved the founding of a Spanish colony west of the Mississippi River. Later he accepted a commission from Citizen Genet, the French representative to the United States, as Commander-in-Chief of the French Revolutionary Legion on the Mississippi. Clark was to enroll an army that would descend the Mississippi and seize Spanish possessions there. But funding was inadequate and the United States forbade the undertaking.

Clark's reputation and ability to conduct business declined so far that he had no significant role in the momentous political events that resulted in Kentucky's statehood in 1792. Nor did one of the state's greatest heroes serve the new commonwealth in any public capacity. Before he reached his fortieth birthday, George Rogers Clark had become a cipher to many of the Kentuckians whom he had served so well in years past.

He lived for several years with his parents in their comfortable Mulberry Hill home. Part of his time was spent in supervising work on the farm; part was devoted to efforts to untangle some of his complicated financial affairs. But he spent many of his hours hunting and riding; he became a close student of nature and of the people who had inhabited Kentucky before the coming of the white man; and he read widely in history and biography.

In 1789, at the urging of such friends as James Madison, Clark began writing his memoirs. He collected a considerable amount of information about his exploits, but he was unable to locate the detailed letter written to George Mason soon after the capture of Vincennes. His interest in the project flagged, and when he stopped writing in 1790 or 1791 he had carried the story little beyond the termination point of the Mason letter. The memoir was, however, surprisingly accurate.

There was still some lingering magic in his name, and faithful friends remembered with respect and admiration the leadership he had once provided. During an Indian scare in 1791 Jefferson asked Judge Harry Innes if it would be possible "to bring Genl. Clark forward. . . . No man alive rated him higher than I did, and would again were he to become again what I knew him." Innes showed the general Jefferson's letter "from a Hope that it might cause him to reflect upon his present folly. He was perfectly sober, was greatly agitated by the contents, observed it was friendly, & shed tears."[5]

Clark retained both his interest in Indian affairs and his belief that there was only one way to settle them. One campaign, he wrote a brother in 1792, "properly directed, would put a final end to the war; and a well-directed line of conduct, after such event should take place, might establish harmony between us and the Indians that might exist for many years."[6] As late as 1794 he harbored some hope that he would be given the command that went to

General Anthony Wayne, but no such call to service came after 1786.

When Clark's parents died in 1799, he was left only a couple of slaves out of the estate, for fear that creditors would seize anything else. The family had decided upon this arrangement, and William Clark interrupted his own career to ease life for his older brother.

An association dear to Clark was his role in supervising the 150,000-acre tract of land set aside for the participants in his Illinois campaign. When the General Assembly established the town of Clarksville across the Ohio from Louisville in October 1783, Clark became one of the trustees. He was also a member and often president of the Board of Commissioners that had charge of the grant. There were many problems in determining eligibility and allocating acres; Clark was present at meetings regularly from 1784 until 1810, when he signed the minutes as president for the last time, and continued to attend when his failing health permitted. The grants, based on rank and length of service, ranged from the 108 acres received by a private to the 8,049 acres that went to Clark. He built a cabin at Clarksville about 1803, where he lived for several years, cared for by two or three family slaves. He failed to establish successful saw- and gristmills, and his dream of digging canals around the Falls remained just that. A visitor who saw him in 1805 commented, "General Clark has become frail and rather helpless, but there are the remains of great dignity and manliness in his countenance, person and deportment."[7] One of his happiest moments came in November 1806, when Meriwether Lewis and William Clark came to see him after completing their great trek to the Pacific northwest. It was a trip that Jefferson, years earlier, had suggested George Rogers Clark make.

In 1809 a stroke left Clark paralyzed in his right side. Then he fell and burned a leg severely in a fireplace, the fall being caused either by his paralysis or his drunkenness, depending upon the source to which one listened. When the wound became infected, surgeons decided to amputate. In the absence of anesthetics, Clark had recourse to martial music. As a young nephew described it, "he sent for the drummer and fifer to come and play. Floyd then took the hint and had all the men placed round the house with two drums and two fifers and played for about two hours and his leg was taken off in the mean time. In the evening they returned and played for about an hour, and then ten at night four elegant violins two drums two fifes marched around the house for about an hour, playing elegant marches."[8]

Then nearly helpless, Clark was finally persuaded to let his family take care of him. He was mentally and physically ill, and his speech became so impaired that even his closest associates had difficulty making out his meaning. By common consent, his relatives agreed to ignore the new will that he insisted on making in 1815. His sister Lucy had married Major William Croghan, and Clark spent his last years at their home, Locust Grove, a few miles east of Louisville. A wheelchair provided some mobility, and a carriage was always available to carry him into town as long as he was able to make the trip. For a time Clark enjoyed hearing from such old friends as Francis Vigo, and he must have derived some belated satisfaction in 1812 from the gift of a sword and a pension of $400 a year from the Virginia legislature. Yet one story reports that when the sword was handed him the old warrior snarled bitterly, "Young man, when Virginia needed a sword, I found her one. Now I need bread!"[9]

Clark attended his last meeting of the Board of Commissioners on February 1, 1813. Then another stroke left him almost totally incapacitated. He lingered on for five more years before dying of apoplexy on February 13, 1818. Five days later he was buried at Locust Grove.

Clark's reputation declined sharply after 1786 because of his own weaknesses and the calumnies circulated by his detractors, and the last thirty years of his life were a bitter anticlimax to his early exploits. Clark operated on a limited scale in a backwater of the Revolution, but he exhibited sagacious foresight in conducting one of the brilliantly conceived and executed campaigns of the American Revolution. Possessed of rare qualities of leadership, Clark inspired his small force by personal example into performing almost incredible feats of endurance and courage that resulted in the conquest of much of the Illinois country. The young commander also displayed an exceptional understanding of psychology and a sound instinct for diplomacy in dealing with the French inhabitants who came under his jurisdiction and the Indian tribes with which he dealt. It is doubtful if anyone of his generation was more successful in dealing with the Indians.

More clearly than most of his contemporaries, Clark recognized the necessity of protecting the Kentucky frontier by carrying the war to the enemy instead of remaining on the defensive. Like a will-o'-the-wisp, Detroit eluded his grasp, but his expeditions north of the Ohio River probably saved the Kentucky settlements from extinction. Had either General Washington or a Virginia governor provided him with one full regiment of regular troops, Clark would probably have captured Detroit and negotiated the Indian peace that did not come until 1795.

Clark's years after the war were a painful postscript to the days of his glory when he earned his reputation as the savior of Kentucky. He lived too long, and his understandable bitterness over his neglect, his flirtations with foreign powers, and his personal excesses all served to tarnish a once glittering reputation. Yet Kentucky owes an eternal debt of gratitude to George Rogers Clark, and Kentuckians would do well to recall the services he rendered the state during the years of its infancy.

In the years after the War of 1812 travelers who passed by Locust Grove sometimes saw the wrecked hulk of a man slumped in a wheelchair. His wasted frame hinted of once great strength, but the vacant eyes gave no indication of the active mind and powerful personality that had once inhabited that body. Paralyzed, a leg amputated, his speech lost, his mind gone, George Rogers Clark lingered on in a twilight existence until death finally released him. But as he waited for that day, as he gazed outwards from Locust Grove, was there ever a moment when he remembered things as they were? Did he still dream of Detroit?

Notes

Chapter 1

1. James Alton James, *The Life of George Rogers Clark* (Chicago, 1928), 23–24.

2. Dale Van Every, *A Company of Heroes: The American Frontier, 1775–1783* (New York, 1962), 63–64.

3. Temple Bodley, *George Rogers Clark, His Life and Public Services* (Boston, 1926), 27.

4. Fannie Casseday Duncan, *When Kentucky Was Young* (Louisville, Ky., 1928), 136.

5. Frederick Palmer, *Clark of the Ohio* (New York, 1930), 90.

6. Clark to Jonathan Clark, July 6, 1775, Draper MSS, 1 L 20 (Wisconsin Historical Society, Madison; microfilm copy at Western Kentucky University, Bowling Green).

7. Clark's Memoir, in James Alton James, ed., *George Rogers Clark Papers*, 2 vols. (Springfield, Ill., 1912, 1924), 1:209.

8. Kathryn Harrod Mason, *James Harrod of Kentucky* (Baton Rouge, La., 1951), 92–93.

9. Consul W. Butterfield, *History of George Rogers Clark's Conquest of the Illinois and the Wabash Towns, 1778 and 1779* (Columbus, Ohio, 1904), 28; Petition of June 20, 1776, in James, ed., *Clark Papers*, 1:14–16.

10. Bodley, *Clark*, 30.

11. William H. English, *Conquest of the Country Northwest of the River Ohio 1778–1783 and Life of Gen. George Rogers Clark*, 2 vols. (Indianapolis, Ind., 1896), 1:75.

12. Bodley, *Clark*, 34.

13. John D. Barnhart, *Henry Hamilton and George Rogers Clark in the American Revolution* (Crawfordsville, Ind., 1951), 29, 30.

14. Charles Gano Talbert, *Benjamin Logan: Kentucky Fron-*

tiersman (Lexington, Ky., 1962), 36; Robert Spencer Cotterill, *History of Pioneer Kentucky* (Cincinnati, Ohio, 1917), 111–12, 120.

15. Butterfield, *Clark's Conquest*, 54–55; Patrick Henry to some County Lieutenants, March 29, 1777, *Official Letters of the Governors of the State of Virginia*, vol. 1, *Letters of Patrick Henry* (Richmond, Va., 1926), 131–32.

16. Julian P. Boyd, ed., *The Papers of Thomas Jefferson* (Princeton, N.J., 1950–), 2:132–33.

17. English, *Clark*, 1:92–93.

18. James, ed., *Clark Papers*, 1:34–36.

Chapter 2

1. Henry to Clark, Jan. 24, 1778, *Official Letters of Henry*, 235; Albert T. Volwiler, *George Croghan and the Westward Movement* (Cleveland, Ohio, 1926), 313.

2. Reuben T. Durrett, *Centenary of Louisville* (Louisville, 1893), 29–30; Clark to James O'Hara, July 15, 1778, in Lawrence Kinnaird, "Clark-Leyba Papers," *American Historical Review* 41 (Oct. 1935): 97.

3. Bodley, *Clark*, 51–52.

4. Fort Ascension, later called Massac, had been built by the French in 1757. It was later abandoned and allowed to fall into ruins. Richard Elwell Banta, *The Ohio* (New York, 1949), 96–97; John Anthony Caruso, *The Great Lakes Frontier* (Indianapolis, Ind., 1961), 41.

5. Mann Butler, *A History of the Commonwealth of Kentucky* (Louisville, Ky., 1834), 53.

6. English, *Clark*, 1:172.

7. de Leyba to Governor General de Galvez, July 21, Oct. 26, and Nov. 16, 1778, in Kinnaird, "Clark-Leyba Papers," 98–102. There is little evidence to support the romantic tale; those who wish to believe have done so.

8. Ross F. Lockridge, *George Rogers Clark, Pioneer Hero of the Old Northwest* (Yonkers-on-the-Hudson, N.Y., 1927), 87–88.

9. Van Every, *Company of Heroes*, 168.

10. John Bakeless, *Background to Glory* (Philadelphia, 1957), 107.

11. C. Herbert Laub, "The Problem of Armed Invasion of the

Northwest during the American Revolution," *Virginia Magazine of History and Biography* 42 (April 1934): 135–36.

12. Wilbur H. Siebert, "Kentucky's Struggle with Its Loyalist Proprietors," *Mississippi Valley Historical Review* 7 (Sept. 1920): 117. This journal will be referred to hereafter as *MVHR*.

Chapter 3

1. John D. Barnhart, "A New Evaluation of Henry Hamilton and George Rogers Clark," *MVHR* 37 (March 1951): 646–48.

2. English, *Clark*, 1:223–24.

3. Barnhart, *Hamilton and Clark*, 29–32, 36, 39–41.

4. James, *Clark*, 110; Butterfield, *Clark's Conquest*, 160; Barnhart, *Hamilton and Clark*, 58.

5. Hamilton's diary is printed in Barnhart, *Hamilton and Clark*.

6. Hamilton said Helm had three Virginians with him; other accounts report only one.

7. Dec. 27, 1778, quoted in Butterfield, *Clark's Conquest*, 244.

8. There is some question whether the crew of the *Willing* was included in the total given for Clark's force. He had either some 130 or 170 men with him on the march. In his "Mason Letter" Clark said he had "upwards of two hundred," but he said 170 in his "Memoir."

9. There is no conclusive proof that Clark personally participated in the killings, although he certainly authorized them. English, *Clark*, 1:342–47.

10. Hambleton Tapp, "George Rogers Clark: A Biographical Sketch," *The Filson Club History Quarterly* 15 (July 1941): 143. This journal will be referred to hereafter as *FCHQ*. Bowman, five other Americans, and a British gunner were injured in an explosion while firing salutes.

Chapter 4

1. Barnhart, *Hamilton and Clark*, chapter 6, relates the harsh treatment Hamilton received as a prisoner in Virginia.

2. Henry to Clark, Dec. 12, 1778, Temple Bodley Collection (The Filson Club, Louisville).

3. Quoted in Butterfield, *Clark's Conquest*, 429, 433.

4. James, ed., *Clark Papers*, 1:304.

5. Draper MSS, 49 J 52. Richard had joined his older brother at Kaskaskia in March 1779.

6. Charles G. Talbert, "Kentucky Invades Ohio, 1779," *Register of the Kentucky Historical Society* 51 (July 1953): 228–33. This journal will be referred to hereafter as *Register*.

7. Clark to Jefferson, Sept. 23, 1779, Boyd, ed., *Papers of Jefferson*, 3:88–89.

8. Jefferson to Washington, June 19, 1779, ibid., 6; Washington to Jefferson, July 10, 1779, John C. Fitzpatrick, ed., *The Writings of George Washington*, 39 vols. (Washington, D.C., 1931–44), 15:401; Washington to Brodhead, Oct. 18, 1779, ibid., 16:486–87.

9. Robert Breckinridge McAfee, "The Life and Times of Robert B. McAfee and His Family and Connections," *Register* 25 (Jan. 1927): 29.

10. Floyd to Col. William Preston, May 5, 1780, Draper MSS, 17 CC 124.

11. William E. Connelley and E. M. Coulter, *History of Kentucky*, 5 vols. (Chicago, 1922), 1:292–93; Temple Bodley, *Our First Great West* (Louisville, Ky., 1938), 199; Clark to father, Aug. 23, 1780, in Temple Bodley, "The National Significance of George Rogers Clark," *MVHR* 11 (Sept. 1924): 177–78.

12. James, *Clark*, 192.

13. Bodley, *Clark*, 163–64.

14. Robert George to Clark, June 4 and July 31, 1780, Bodley Collection.

15. Washington to Jefferson, Oct. 10 and Dec. 28, 1780, Boyd, ed., *Papers of Jefferson*, 4:28, 246–47; Jefferson to Crockett, Sept. 27, 1780, ibid., 3:667; Jefferson to Washington, Dec. 13, 1780, ibid., 4:204–6; Washington to Brodhead, Dec. 29, 1780, Fitzpatrick, ed., *Writings of Washington*, 21:33–35.

16. Jefferson to Clark, Dec. 25, 1780, Boyd, ed., *Papers of Jefferson*, 4:233–37.

17. Clark to Jefferson, Jan. 18, 1781, *Calendar of Virginia State Papers*, 11 vols. (Richmond, 1875–1893), 1:441. The *Calendar* will be referred to hereafter as *CVSP*.

18. Officers of Berkeley County Militia to Jefferson, Jan. 25, 1781, Boyd, ed., *Papers of Jefferson*, 4:451–52.

19. Montgomery to Governor, Aug. 10, 1781, *CVSP*, 2:313; Todd to Jefferson, April 16, 1781, Boyd, ed., *Papers of Jefferson*, 5:467.

20. Clark to Jefferson, Aug. 4, 1781, James, ed., *Clark Papers*, 1:578.

21. Floyd to Jefferson, April 16, 1781, *CVSP*, 2:49; Floyd to Clark, Aug. 10, 1781, Draper MSS, 51 J 80.

22. English, *Clark*, 2:737–38; *CVSP*, 2:192–93; Boyd, ed., *Papers of Jefferson*, 5:599; Captain John Baley to Clark, Aug. 6, 1781, quoted in English, *Clark*, 2:747.

23. Slaughter to Governor, Aug. 9, 1781, *CVSP*, 2:306.

24. Draper MSS, 51 J 84.

25. James, ed., *Clark Papers*, 1:608.

Chapter 5

1. James A. James, "Appraisal of the Contributions of George Rogers Clark to the History of the West," *MVHR* 17 (June 1930):108.

2. Talbert, *Logan*, 163–66; Charles G. Talbert, "A Roof for Kentucky," *FCHQ* 29 (April 1955):157–58; *CVSP*, 3:281–82.

3. Boone to Governor, Aug. 30, 1782, *CVSP*, 3:275–76.

4. *CVSP*, 3:337.

5. Quoted in Bodley, *Clark*, 215–16.

6. Clark to Governor, Oct. 18, 1782, *CVSP*, 3:345.

7. Quoted in James, "Appraisal of Clark," 110.

8. Jan. 13, 1783, James, ed., *Clark Papers*, 2:181–82.

9. *CVSP*, 3:386; Draper MSS, 52 J 50.

10. *CVSP*, 3:384–87; Harrison to Clark, Dec. 19, 1782, Harrison Letter Book, Bodley Collection.

11. *CVSP*, 3:453.

12. Clark to Col. William Davies, Jan. 1, 1783, Bodley Collection; *CVSP*, 3:437.

13. *CVSP*, 3:448, 477.

14. Talbert, "Roof for Kentucky," 162; Francis S. Philbrick, *The Rise of the West* (New York, 1965), 75; Christopher Ward, *The War of the Revolution*, 2 vols. (New York, 1952), 2:865; Caruso, *Great Lakes Frontier*, 81–83; Lewis J. Carey, "Benjamin Franklin Is Informed of Clark's Activities in the Old Northwest," *MVHR* 21 (Dec. 1934):375, 378.

15. May 21, 1783, *CVSP*, 3:487.

Chapter 6

1. *CVSP*, 4:122.
2. Bodley, *Clark*, 281–82.
3. Draper MSS, 23 J 163.
4. James, *Clark*, 376–78.
5. Bodley, *Clark*, 343–44.
6. English, *Clark*, 2:788–89.
7. Palmer, *Clark*, 461.
8. Quoted in James, *Clark*, 467. Floyd was Clark's namesake, Colonel George Rogers Clark Floyd, son of Clark's friend John Floyd.
9. Bodley, *Clark*, 372.

A Note to Readers

A GREAT MASS of information, much of it contemporary with its subject, is available on George Rogers Clark. Lyman C. Draper collected materials over several decades for a biography he never wrote; the Clark Papers constitute the largest collection in the Draper Manuscripts (State Historical Society of Wisconsin, Madison). A microfilm copy of these papers at Western Kentucky University was used in this study. Temple Bodley also collected extensively from many depositories in preparation for his biography of Clark; his large collection is in The Filson Club (Louisville). Most of the Clark papers dating from before 1785 (including Clark's Harrodsburg diary) were published in *George Rogers Clark Papers*, ed. James Alton James, 2 vols. (Springfield, Ill., 1912–1926). The validity of Clark's most important writings is examined in James A. James, "Value of the Memoir of George Rogers Clark as an Historical Document," *MVHR* 5 (Oct. 1918):249–70, and Temple Bodley, "Clark's 'Mason Letter' and 'Memoir,'" *FCHQ* 3 (July 1929):163–70.

A number of useful letters are in Julian P. Boyd, ed., *The Papers of Thomas Jefferson*, 19 vols. to date (Princeton, N.J., 1950–); John C. Fitzpatrick, ed., *The Writings of George Washington*, 39 vols. (Washington, D.C., 1931–44); *Calendar of Virginia State Papers*, vols. 1–5 (Richmond, 1875–1885); and Lawrence Kinnaird, "Clark-Leyba Papers," *American Historical Review* 41 (Oct. 1935):92–112. Robert A. Rutland, ed., *The Papers of George Mason*, 2 vols. to date (Chapel Hill, N.C., 1970–), is disappointing in view of Clark's close friendship with Mason.

The best biographies of Clark are James Alton James, *The Life of George Rogers Clark* (Chicago, 1928); Temple Bodley, *George Rogers Clark, His Life and Public Services* (Boston, 1926); William H. English, *Conquest of the Country Northwest of the River Ohio 1778–1783 and Life of Gen. George Rogers Clark*, 2 vols. (Indianapolis, Ind., 1896); and John Bakeless, *Background to Glory* (Philadelphia, 1957). The Bodley and English volumes contain a great deal of primary material. A good brief sketch is Hambleton Tapp, "George Rogers Clark, A Biographical Sketch," *FCHQ* 15 (July 1941):133–51. Less adequate biographies include Consul W. Butterfield, *History of George Rogers Clark's Conquest of the Illinois and the Wabash Towns, 1778 and 1779* (Columbus, Ohio, 1904); Walter Havighurst, *George Rogers Clark, Soldier in the West* (New York, 1952); Ross F. Lockridge, *George Rogers Clark, Pioneer Hero of the Old Northwest* (Yonkers-on-the-Hudson, N.Y., 1927); and Frederick Palmer, *Clark of the Ohio* (New York, 1930). Earlier biographies are discussed in Louise Phelps Kellogg, "The Early Biographers of George Rogers Clark," *American Historical Review* 35 (Jan. 1930):295–302.

Excellent introductions to the early history of Kentucky are Otis K. Rice, *Frontier Kentucky* (Lexington, Ky., 1975), and Thomas D. Clark, *A History of Kentucky* (Lexington, Ky., 1960). Robert Spencer Cotterill, *History of Pioneer Kentucky* (Cincinnati, Ohio, 1917), is anti-Clark. Humphrey Marshall's *History of Kentucky* (Frankfort, Ky., 1812), and Mann Butler's *A History of the Commonwealth of Kentucky* (Louisville, Ky., 1834) have special significance because the authors were personally acquainted with the Clark era in the state's history. Lewis Collins and Richard H. Collins, *History of Kentucky*, 2 vols. (Covington, Ky., 1874), has a great deal of information, especially in its "Annals." All of the comprehensive histories of the state devote considerable attention both to Clark and to the Revolutionary period.

Charles Gano Talbert, *Benjamin Logan: Kentucky Frontiersman* (Lexington, Ky., 1962), is a fine objective biography of one of Clark's frequent associates. Other useful biographies are: John Bakeless, *Daniel Boone* (New York, 1939); Kathryn Harrod Mason, *James Harrod of Kentucky* (Baton Rouge, La., 1951); James Alton James, *Oliver Pollock* (New York, 1937); Edna Kenton, *Simon Kenton* (Garden City, N.Y., 1930); and Patricia Jahns, *The Violent Years: Simon Kenton and the Ohio-Kentucky Frontier* (New York, 1962). Robert Breckinridge McAfee, "The Life and Times of Robert B. McAfee and His Family and Connections," *Register* 25 (Jan., May, Sept. 1927): 5–37, 111–43, 215–37, has some fascinating accounts of life in pioneer Kentucky.

The best general introduction to the American Revolution is Don Higginbotham, *The War of American Independence* (New York, 1971), but Christopher Ward, *The War of the Revolution*, 2 vols. (New York, 1952), is more complete on military aspects of the conflict. Dale Van Every has written two good popular accounts of the West during this era: *Men of the Western Waters* (Boston, 1956), and *A Company of Heroes* (New York, 1962). Also helpful for general surveys are Jack M. Sosin, *The Revolutionary Frontier, 1763–1783* (New York, 1967); Temple Bodley, *Our First Great West* (Louisville, Ky., 1938); and Francis S. Philbrick, *The Rise of the West, 1754–1830* (New York, 1965). The two major routes into Kentucky during Clark's period are described in Richard Elwell Banta, *The Ohio* (New York, 1949), and Robert L. Kincaid, *The Wilderness Road* (Indianapolis, Ind., 1947).

Numerous studies have been made of Clark's battles and campaigns. John D. Barnhart, *Henry Hamilton and George Rogers Clark in the American Revolution* (Crawfordsville, Ind., 1951), contains Hamilton's journal. The capture of one of the most important Illinois towns has been well described in Milo Milton Quaife, *The Capture of Old Vincennes* (Indianapolis, Ind., 1927), and August Derleth, *Vincennes: Portal to the West* (Englewood Cliffs, N.J., 1968). Quaife, *The Conquest of the Illinois* (Chicago, 1920), includes Clark's "Memoir" in addition to a general discussion of the campaign. Charles G. Talbert has written a series of excellent articles on military expeditions of this period for the *Register:* "Kentucky Invades Ohio, 1779," 51 (July 1953):228–35; "Kentucky Invades Ohio, 1780," 52 (Oct. 1954):291–300; "Kentucky Invades Ohio, 1782," 53 (Oct. 1955):288-97; and "Kentucky Invades Ohio, 1786," 54 (July 1956):203–13. One should also read Talbert's article "A Roof for Kentucky," *FCHQ* 29 (April 1955):145–65. Older but still useful are Milo M. Quaife, "When Detroit Invaded Kentucky," *FCHQ* 1 (Jan. 1927):53–67, and "The Ohio Campaigns of 1782," *MVHR* 17 (March 1931):515–29.

Numerous articles deal with Clark and the war in the West. In addition to those already cited, one should read John D. Barnhart, "A New Evaluation of Henry Hamilton and George Rogers Clark," *MVHR* 37 (March 1951):643–52; James Alton James, "Appraisal of the Contributions of George Rogers Clark to the History of the West," *MVHR* 17 (June 1930):98–115; Wilbur H. Siebert, "Kentucky's Struggle with Its Loyalist Proprietors," *MVHR* 7 (Sept. 1920):113–26; and Patricia Watlington, "Discontent in Frontier Kentucky," *Register* 65 (April 1967):77–93. It will be noted that much of the writing about Clark appeared before the Second World War; he has been comparatively neglected for the last thirty years.